Letters to the Homeland
An Accurate Translation of an Intimate Voice

By Andrea Emily Stumpf

Translating the original turn-of-the-century
Briefe nach der Heimat
from her great-great-grandmother,

Emily Ruete,
born Sayyida Salme bint Said bin Sultan Al Bu Said,
Princess of Oman and Zanzibar

Copyright © 2023 Andrea E. Stumpf
First edition; published in the United States, 2023
Cover design: Andrea E. Stumpf
Copy Editor: Lauri Scherer, LSF Editorial
Graphic Designer: Joe Bernier, Bernier Graphics

Andrea E. Stumpf has asserted her right as copyright owner of this publication, including under the Copyright, Designs and Patents Act of 1988, to be identified as the author of this work, including as translator of the translated text contained herein. Max S. Stumpf is the copyright owner of the illustrations appearing on pages 3, 15, 28, 53, 87, 97, and 121.

The original text that has been translated for this publication comes from handwritten documents from Sayyida Salme/Emily Ruete, along with a later typed version, entitled *Briefe nach der Heimat*. Compiled as part of the *Literarischer Nachlass* (literary estate) of Sayyida Salme/Emily Ruete, her son Rudolph Said-Ruete granted the documents to the Oriental Institute in Leiden in 1937, along with his own collected books and materials. This special collection was then moved as a permanent loan to the Netherlands Institute for the Near East (NINO) in 1977 and became part of the Leiden University Libraries in 2018 as the Said Ruete Archive, Or. 27.135.

All rights reserved. No part of this book may be reproduced, translated, or transmitted in any form or by any means, electronic or hard copy, including photocopying, recording, by any storage or retrieval system, or otherwise, without prior written permission of the author, translator, and copyright owner. For permission, send a request with complete information to andrea@sayyidasalme.com.

www.sayyidasalme.com; www.emilyruete.com

ISBN 978-1-7323975-5-2

Dedicated to my dearest, devoted mother,
Ursula Emily Stumpf.

When mothers and daughters collaborate,
I hear history rhyme.

This book is presented as a sequel to *Memoirs of an Arabian Princess: An Accurate Translation of Her Authentic Voice*, also by Andrea Emily Stumpf, the author's great-great-granddaughter. All references to the *"Memoirs"* in footnotes and elsewhere in this book are to this version of the *Memoirs*.

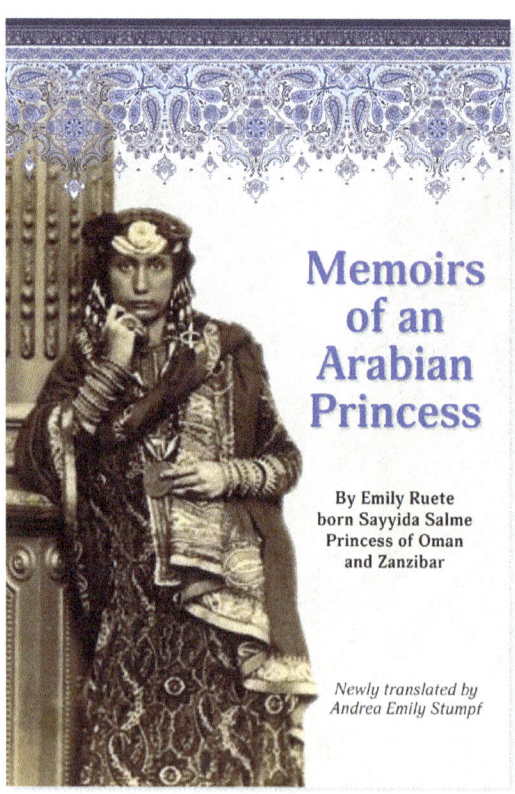

CONTENTS

Introduction:

About Sayyida Salme vi

About the Manuscript xx

Letters to the Homeland

— translated from the original German —

pages 1 to 120

From the translator:

Map of Places Lived 121

On Collaboration 126

On Freedom 129

On Fear 135

On Inspiration 140

List of Abbreviations 152

Timeline 153

List of Images 160

ABOUT SAYYIDA SALME

Because she wrote her own story, there is less for me to say. Sayyida Salme, who later became Emily Ruete, published *Memoiren einer arabischen Prinzessin* in 1886, which I newly translated in 2022 as *Memoirs of an Arabian Princess: An Accurate Translation of Her Authentic Voice*. She also wrote *Briefe nach der Heimat* in subsequent years, which you now have here, newly translated in 2023 as *Letters to the Homeland: An Accurate Translation of an Intimate Voice*.

Sayyida Salme began her life in Zanzibar, born into the Omani Sultanate that ruled the island. Her father was the Sultan, and her mother was a *surie* from the Circassian diaspora. So much of that remarkable time and place would have faded into the past were it not for the generous details Sayyida Salme shared with us in her *Memoirs*. And now with her *Letters*, she gives us a whole new perspective, a deeper, more dismal view of her life in the West. In the aftermath of her fateful decision—if it was fate—we realize that she never really left the island, or at least, the island never left her. We also see that she never really settled into her new home, with much to unsettle her along the way. Geographically, socially, spiritually, at every level, she found herself straddling two worlds, but secure in neither.

If I dare sum up her long life in two points, it was her learning to write at the end of her first decade and her choice of husband at the end of her second decade that defined her the most, even into the present. Already inclined to bump up against the sides of the box, in these two points she breached the confines, by learning a taboo skill and choosing a taboo husband. With the latter, at the same time that explorers from the West were "discovering" the East, including East Africa, she uniquely became the reverse: a probing and insightful explorer from the East (including as an Arab) of the West. With the former, through her writing, she acquired the tools to record her remote setting, reveal spaces hidden from view, share thoughts and critiques, stay in touch with her homeland, and most importantly, capture words on a page for us to study, enjoy, criticize, and contemplate—notably, as the first Arab woman to publish a book.

About Sayyida Salme

Although she used the name Emily Ruete for most of her life, I choose to refer to her as Sayyida Salme.[1] I do not know if she would approve, since she took the name Ruete out of lasting love and devotion to her husband, and she was endeared to her namesake Emily Seward, the British consul's wife who helped her flee. Then again, she included her Arabic name on the cover of her *Memoirs*, and her family added this appellation to the cover page of her *Letters*. What motivates me above all, however, are the circumstances of her name change. When she gave up her name, she gained her husband, but also had to give up so much more. I see her Western name as yet another coercive element that she had to accept in her chosen life, in which so many choices were met with so much lack of choice. I reach back to her original name, wanting to connect with her deep down inside, and feel grateful for how much more choice we have today.

Whatever moved her to write, we are the beneficiaries. She left a legacy of recollection and remembrance that still speaks to us. The world is her audience, and the relevance of her life and writing still resonates.

Andrea Emily Stumpf,
her great-great-granddaughter

---

1 "Sayyida" has a particular meaning in Oman, not to be confused with the usual Islamic reference to a descendant of the prophet Muhammed. "Sayyida" for Princess, and "Sayyid" for Prince or Sultan, denotes a member of the Al Bu Said royal family, a hereditary honorific through paternal lineage without religious connotation. The author's father preferred the title "Sayyid" and expressly set aside the religious title "Imam" of his forebears to which he and his family were entitled. Omani Ibadism allowed for this separation between Imamate and Sultanate. As for his full name, Sayyid Said bin Sultan, Sayyid is equivalent to "Sultan," whereas Sultan was, in fact, the first name of his father, Sayyid Sultan bin Ahmed.

The author, Hamburg, ca. 1868.

The author, Hamburg, ca. 1868.

The author, Hamburg, ca. 1868.

The author, Hamburg, ca. 1868.

The author, Hamburg, ca. 1868.

The author, Hamburg, ca. 1868.

The author, Berlin, 1888.

The author, Berlin, 1888.

The author, 1908.

The author, 1908.

The author, Beirut, between 1892–1914.

The author, Bromberg (now Bydgoszcz), 1914.

ABOUT THE MANUSCRIPT

Briefe nach der Heimat, literally translated "Letters to the Homeland," is the title that Emily Ruete, born Sayyida Salme, gave her own manuscript. Whether the contents came from actual letters is unclear. Perhaps the text was transcribed from individual letters and melded into a single, end-to-end account. Perhaps letters, as such, were never meant to be sent, but rather served as a literary device to unleash her recollections. We have only her handwritten manuscript, without any documented history of its provenance, no original letters or prior drafts. In its pages, we do not in fact see letters. To pick up the original is to see one long rendition, without to and from and dates, without even paragraphs or indentations—merely the occasional stroke of a line to separate topics, as if to take a quick breath before rushing on.

Even so, the label "letters" rings true. The tone of Sayyida Salme's account is familiar, interspersed with frequent references to "you" that speak directly to someone in Zanzibar.[2] The presentation is knowing and personal, addressed to someone close to her, someone who grew up with her and drew from common experiences, who knew her jewelry, her moods, her values. It feels like the author is writing a kindred spirit, an intimate soulmate—this someone who owned a plantation, journeyed to Mecca, and was jealous of a pretty white cat. Across from the author, we sense someone expecting to hear from her, awaiting her news, and sharing in return.

In this literary work, the passages seemingly pour out of her—*in einem Guß,* in one flow, as we say in German. The visual effect is stunning, with long cursive lines that course across page after page. The author gives us an unbroken stream of scenes and stories of her painfully broken life, as if to play on her lifelong theme of perseverance. She fills three volumes of black on white handwriting, both front and back on thin paper, traversing more than six hundred pages in all. This is the trail of a long run, an uphill climb, an exhausting marathon—a narrative that marks one excruciating, extenuating episode after another. So much to say, to recount, to fathom, even as we know details are being left out, and the end leaves us hanging.[3]

---

[2] This starts with the very first sentence, which calls out a *geliebte Freundin,* a dear female friend. Sayyida Salme also tells us that she corresponded with "loyal friends" she left behind in Zanzibar, although there is no known record of these letters, either coming or going. See A.E. Stumpf, *Memoirs of an Arabian Princess: An Accurate Translation of Her Authentic Voice,* p. 36 (2022) (hereinafter *Memoirs*).

[3] We can still find ample meaning in her closing words, as I do in my essay "On Fear" on pages 135–39 below.

About the Manuscript

As lengthy as the work is, and as searing the detail, Sayyida Salme kept it to herself. Even the author's three children were seemingly unaware of this heart-wrenching account until she died. Their discovery of the manuscript among her belongings after she passed away on February 29, 1924, was surely shocking. No matter that the family had been so close, no matter how much the children thought they knew their mother, this found text presented a new level of intimacy and anguish. As one daughter wrote to her brother: "Her martyrdom was hard—it is shattering to read through her literary legacy."[4]

What to do with them, these three volumes marked only I, II, and III? Tony, Said, and Rosa[5] (the latter being my direct ancestor) immediately registered their importance. As the first Arab woman to have published a book, to great interest and popular acclaim, who had also written another piece in close collaboration with her children,[6] the author's voice was already out there, her intention to share more of her struggles had been clear, and here was another dimension of her life that was hard to ignore. To make this part of her public legacy or not—that was the question. The children exchanged differing views amongst themselves, but in the end, the view that this substantial text deserved to be shared with the world apparently prevailed. Tucked in at page 16 of the family's copy of Lionel Strachey's unauthorized[7] translation of the *Memoiren* are several letters dated 1925, documenting overtures that were

---

4 *Ihr Martyrium was schwer—beim Durchlesen ihres Nachlasses ist man erschüttert*. Rosa Troemer writing to her brother Rudolph Said-Ruete on June 15, 1924. Leiden University Libraries Or. 27.135 C5(2).
5 Tony is what Antonie (also Thawka) was called; Said was called by his second name (men in the Ruete family appear to have been called by their second names), until he later chose to be called by his first name, Rudolph; and Rosa is what Rosalie (also Ghuza) was called.
6 Evidencing this interaction, the *Nachtrag zu meinen Memoiren* (Addendum to My Memoirs), primarily about the circumstances of the author's 1888 trip to Zanzibar, consists of two notebooks of draft text that are preserved in the Leiden University Libraries: one in the author's hand, with handwritten edits primarily by her daughter Rosa (Or. 27.135 A1), and one in Rosa's hand, with handwritten edits likely by the author's son Rudolph (Or. 27.135 A2).
7 It seems clear that Lionel Strachey took it upon himself to issue a translation of the *Memoiren* without consulting or collaborating with the author or her family, based on two pieces of evidence, in particular. First, his edition is a significant misrepresentation of the original, in which Strachey took great license in revising the author's original text, including adding his own subheaders, merging and dropping chapters, and inserting misleading photographic images. The continuing popularity of this inaccurate and abridged distortion of her original publication is a major reason I decided to publish my version of the *Memoiren*, which I had translated as accurately as possible, as much as a translation can be. Second, one can readily deduce that the family itself had concerns about Strachey's edition from the fact that Rudolph had loosely inserted a clipped article from the London *Times* dated March 31, 1928, at the title page of Strachey's book (Leiden University Libraries SR 618). Entitled "America and the Law of Copyright," it discussed copyright rules in the United States after Congress failed to pass much-needed legislation. According to the article, "The difficulty which has principally confronted both English and American authors … has not in fact been actual piracy … so much as the willful inconveniences of the present system." Against this backdrop, there was apparently little the family could do to remedy the situation and redirect attention to the family-authorized edition that had been collaboratively produced with London's Ward & Downey in 1888.

made to two English publishers, but turned down.[8] One can perhaps surmise that unsuccessful overtures were also made to one or more German publishing houses. Even in the years after that, some of the children, and later some of their descendants, vacillated between leaving history alone and drawing attention to this remarkable story.[9]

It was not until Professor Emeri van Donzel published his impressive 1993 compilation of the author's literary works, which included his newly translated "Letters Home," that an English version of this text saw the light of day.[10] Not long after, Heinz Schneppen, the German Ambassador to Tanzania from 1993 to 1996, was the first to publish the *Briefe nach der Heimat* in the original German.[11] With an English version of the *Letters* nestled in an academic volume that is superb but pricey, and with the original German version offered in another book that has long been out of print, it is not clear how much currency this illuminating document has received to date, but it deserves more.

———•———

As to my own work, as Sayyida Salme's great-great-granddaughter, this new translation you have in your hands, or on your screen, or in your ears, is the sequel to my newly translated *Memoirs of an Arabian Princess*. The two books make a meaningful pair, one primarily about the author's early life in Zanzibar, the other primarily about her later life in Germany. But that is too neatly stated. The push-and-pull of her straddled existence is evident in both texts. She writes from an emerging German perspective when recounting her life in Zanzibar. She addresses her thoughts via a Zanzibari perspective when detailing her life in Germany. This ability to hold the two in one hand is a gift to us, but was, in so many ways, raw agony for her.

---

8 Both William Heinemann Limited of London and Doubleday, Page and Company of New York reviewed the *Briefe nach der Heimat* manuscript provided by the author's son Rudolph, but declined to publish. See letters placed by Rudolph in the book located at Leiden University Libraries SR 618.
9 Rosa, who had a close working relationship with her mother, took the latter view: "The main thing is to preserve the memory of someone of mother's importance." (*Das Wesentliche ist, eine Persönlichkeit von Mutters Ausmaß dem Gedächtnis zu erhalten.*) Rosa writing to her brother Rudolph in January 1928, according to H. Schneppen, *Emily Ruete geb. Prinzessin Salme von Oman und Sansibar: Briefe nach der Heimat*, p. 7 (1999) (hereinafter H. Schneppen, *Briefe*).
10 E. van Donzel, *An Arabian Princess Between Two Worlds: Memoirs, Letters, Sequels to the Memoirs, Syrian Customs and Usages*, pp. 407–510 (1993) (hereinafter E. van Donzel). As Professor van Donzel explained to me, he had initially intended to publish the original German texts, but was unexpectedly preempted by Professor Annegret Nippa, who had published the *Memoiren* in German a few years before, thus causing him to shift to English. Ibid., Preface at p. ix, referring to A. Nippa, *Leben im Sultanspalast* (1989).
11 H. Schneppen, *Briefe*.

About the Manuscript

From a timing perspective, these two accounts, the *Memoirs* and the *Letters*, are, roughly speaking, her BE and AE, the before and after elopement and self-exile. Only the tail end of her *Memoirs* takes place after Sayyida Salme left Zanzibar, and none of the *Letters* takes place before she left. The two were also written sequentially. The *Memoirs* were started in the mid-1870s,[12] and the *Letters* were started only after the *Memoirs* came out in 1886.[13] In the *Memoirs*, we are simply given a short, two-page, rather positive AE picture of the first dozen or so years in Germany, with merely a hint of difficulty.[14] The *Letters* then lift the lid and let loose her truth.

Indeed, it is almost jaw-dropping to realize that Sayyida Salme was living much of the agonizing period described in her *Letters* at the same time she was writing the *Memoirs*. During those years, in her early thirties, she was so critically at the end of her rope that it seems almost implausible for her to have been writing on the side. But she admits in the *Memoirs* that she felt time-bound and needed to write about her past while she could.[15] She also tantalizingly tells us in the *Memoirs* that she may share more about her "first impressions of European life and customs of the civilized world."[16] This may well refer to what later became the *Letters*. For the reverse, however, nothing in the *Letters* mentions the *Memoirs* that she was creating during the years she describes.

---

12 It makes sense that Sayyida Salme would have felt the urge to hold onto her history after the children, in their first days of public schooling in 1877, became aware of her unusual ancestry (below at page 98). Or she may have started writing the *Memoirs* earlier, after failing to reconnect with Sultan Barghash in London in 1875, which is the year cited by Professor van Donzel. E. van Donzel, p. 1.

13 As to when the author wrote her *Letters*, the exact dates are unknown. The opening line indicates that she is finally responding after a long silence, looking back years later. Extrapolating from her mention of Sultan Barghash's death in 1888 (below at page 71), the manuscript may well have originated after the author's second trip to Zanzibar that same year, during her time in Jaffa (now part of Tel Aviv) (1888–1892) or Beirut (1892–1914). By then, her children were of age, and she presumably had more time and space of mind to put her memories and thoughts to paper. But it was likely also completed before she wrote her original last will and testament in 1910. There she addresses both her *Memoirs* and "the as-yet unpublished manuscripts that describe my life in Europe," the latter possibly, at least in part, a reference to the *Letters* manuscript.

14 "[M]isfortune continued to pursue me." *Memoirs*, p. 203.

15 "Physically and emotionally spent, I did not expect to last long enough to see them into adulthood to then tell them about my fateful journey and childhood memories. I therefore decided to write up my experiences and undertook the project with great love and dedication, knowing it was for my dear children, whose tenderness had comforted me during long and troubled years, and whose deep empathy has sustained me through my trying times." *Memoirs*, Preface, p. 1

16 "I have written up these impressions in reverent memory [of my late husband] and may find a subsequent opportunity to report on them as well." *Memoirs*, p. 202.

Readers of the *Memoirs* may be surprised by the *Letters*; it is not what you would expect. The *Memoirs* are as light in tone and style as the *Letters* are dark. How could she have been living under such trauma and duress without letting that permeate her writing of the *Memoirs*? It surely took focus and discipline to convey the special, happy, carefree childhood she had had on the island, without dwelling on the present—or maybe it was some degree of disassociation. Writing a book for children, her own children for them to remember her by, would have been reason enough to hold back on her sentiments. And then later, it may have been all the more necessary to channel her dire truth, to unload her part two. With the *Memoirs*, she may not have wanted to burden her children right away, but with the *Letters*, she knew they would, one day, read the rest of her story.

In developing this new translation, I was able to draw from three sources of the author's *Briefe nach der Heimat*. First is the original text I described above, of which you can get a sense in the photographs right after this essay. While beautiful in its flow, the handwritten use of the old Sütterlin script makes it challenging to read (unless you are my mother). Second is a carefully preserved, typewritten manuscript of 181 pages as part of the historical collection kept by Antonie's branch of the family, to which I was given gracious access by my third cousin, Alexander von Brand. It turns out he lives near us in the Washington, DC, area, as did his grandmother, who knew and interacted with my German grandfather, although that connection got lost and was only recently rekindled (with thanks to Anita Keizers and Godwin Kornes).

Third is a subsequently typewritten manuscript of 177 pages that resides at the Leiden University Libraries Or. 6281. It was formally presented by the author's son Rudolph to the Oriental Institute in Leiden in 1929,[17] shortly after the Institute was founded by Professor Christiaan Snouck Hurgronje, a close friend of the family.[18] Perhaps showing some sensitivity for the nature

---

17 Copies of this typewritten text were also formally sent to the Zanzibar Museum in Stone Town, the British Museum in London, the Staats- and Universitätsbibliothek in Hamburg, and the Preussische Staatsbibliothek in Berlin, per correspondence at Leiden University Libraries Or. 25.137 C8.
18 Professor Hurgronje also welcomed Rudolph's subsequent interest in providing his extensive private library to the Oriental Institute. Over six hundred books and other documents relating to the history of Oman and Zanzibar, Middle Eastern politics (especially the question of Palestine), and much of his mother's legacy, including letters, photographs, and other personal documents, made their way to Leiden in 1937, one year after Professor Hurgronje died.

About the Manuscript

of the narrative, or maybe just to keep control, Rudolph stipulated that his mother's *Briefe nach der Heimat* could not be published before 1940. This third copy corrects a number of grammatical and other minor errors in the prior typewritten copy, but otherwise leaves the tract intact. I used primarily this third copy for my translation, cross-checking with the two earlier versions as needed.

Since the original manuscript was a posthumous find, the children had no opportunity to work with their mother to get her text in good shape for a book. And so it remains, one or more drafts shy of a polished publication, unlike the *Memoirs*. To my mind, that makes the *Letters* more poignant, more unabashed. What may feel like repetition actually reflects the tenacity of certain topics. What comes across as a lack of structure is, in fact, true to the endless stream of life. I appreciate this unvarnished account as the unedited real deal.

In translating, I have hewn to the original as much as possible, barring a few added subdividers and lots of paragraph breaks, all marked, to help pace the reader. The footnotes and accompanying essays are all mine. For these, my work has benefited from many other documents, including those assembled and annotated over the years by Rudolph for his private collection. The special bookcase he provided to house this collection is no longer filled,[19] since its varied contents now rest more comfortably in climate-controlled vaults. But even now, these materials remain a treasure trove for anyone who wishes to delve deeper and discover more.[20]

Andrea Emily Stumpf
September 2023

---

19 *Memoirs*, "On Contributions," p. 232.
20 We are grateful that Leiden University and the Netherlands Institute for the Near East (NINO) continue to safeguard these materials, while also making them available to the public. A useful description of this history and itemization of some of the collection appears in the Leiden University Libraries' collection guide (at ubl649) of the Sayyida Salme (Emily Ruete) and Rudolph Said-Ruete archive from 2018 that was excellently prepared by Hans van de Velde and Arnoud Vrolijk.

The author's handwritten manuscript, three filled notebooks.

Cover page followed by pages 1, 2, and 3 of each notebook.

BRIEFE NACH DER HEIMAT.

Wie oft batest Du mich geliebte Freundin, ich sollte Dir doch ausfurliches ueber meine Erlebnisse im Norden berichten. Wenn das bis jetzt nicht ganz zu Deiner Zufriedenheit geschah, so lag das meist daran, dass ich hauptsaechlich mich vor dem Erlebten fast fuertete, noch einmal in Einzelheiten im Geiste alles wieder durchzumachen. Auch bin ich keineswegs sicher, ob ich Deinem Wunsche im Ganzen und Grossen, hauptsaechlich aber zu Deiner Zufriedenheit gerecht werden kann. Denn das Leben, Sitten, Gebrauche und Anschauungen der Nordlander sind so himmelhoch verschieden vo den unsereigen dass ich befurchten muss, es konnte Dir manches ubertrieben, ja selbst vielleicht unmoglich erscheinen. Ging es denn mir selbst von Anfang auch aders, wo ich doch lebhaftig in deren Mitten versetzt wurde? Jahre brauchte ich, um aus der stillen Verwunderung heraus zu kommen, von all dem was mich umgab und was ich im Laufe der Zeit zu sehen und zu horen bekam. Denn die Erfindungsgabe der Menschen hier im Durchschnitt ist ganz erstaunlich. Sie stehen jedenfalls in ihrere Geistigen Leistung oben an. Dagegen sind sie aber auch - fur unsere - etwas gar zu prosaisch, so dass unser einem nicht leicht wird, sich in ihre Anschauungen hineinzu denken. Dem Fremdling gegenuber sind sie im allgemeinem zuvorkommend; iher Antipoden vor

First typewritten version of the author's manuscript.

BRIEFE NACH DER HEIMAT.

Wie oft batest Du mich, geliebte Freundin, ich sollte Dir doch Ausführliches über meine Erlebnisse im Norden berichten. Wenn das bis jetzt nicht ganz zu Deiner Zufriedenheit geschah, so lag das meist daran, dass ich hauptsächlich mich vor dem Erlebten fast fürchtete, noch einmal in Einzelheiten im Geiste alles wieder durchzumachen. Auch bin ich keineswegs sicher, ob ich Deinem Wunsche im grossen und ganzen, hauptsächlich aber zu Deiner Zufriedenheit gerecht werden kann, denn das Leben, die Sitten, Gebräuche und Anschauungen der Nordländer sind so himmelhoch verschieden von den unsrigen, dass ich befürchten muss, es könnte Dir manches übertrieben, ja selbst vielleicht unmöglich erscheinen. Ging es denn mir selbst im Anfang anders, wo ich doch leibhaftig in deren Mitte versetzt wurde? Jahre brauchte ich, um aus der stillen Verwunderung herauszukommen von all dem, was mich umgab und was ich im Laufe der Zeit zu sehen und zu hören bekam. Denn die Erfindungsgabe der Menschen hier im Durchschnitt ist ganz erstaunlich. Sie stehen jedenfalls in ihrer geistigen Leistung obenan. Dagegen sind sie aber auch - für unsere Begriffe - etwas gar zu prosaisch, so dass es unser einem nicht leicht wird, sich in ihre Anschauungen hineinzudenken. Dem Fremdling gegenüber sind sie im allgemeinen zuvorkommend; ihre Antipoden vor allem erfreuen sich stets ihrer Aufmerksamkeit und Teilnahme. Demgegenüber tritt aber dem Neuling überall der vorherrschende Realismus so mächtig entgegen, dass er unwillkürlich und aus Mangel an Verständnis die Zuflucht nur in sich

Second typewritten version of the author's manuscript.

Literarischer Nachlass

von

EMILY RUETE

(Seyyidah Salme bint Said bin Sultan)

geb. 30. August 1844 in Zansibar,

gest. 29. Februar 1924 in Jena.

In Ergänzung

der

"Memoiren einer Arabischen Prinzessin."

Berlin 1886.

Translated:

Literary Estate of *EMILY RUETE* (Seyyidah Salme bint Said bin Sultan), born August 30, 1844, in Zanzibar, died February 29, 1924, in Jena.

As a supplement to the "Memoirs of an Arabian Princess," Berlin 1886.

All footnotes in the following pages were added by the translator.

Letters to the Homeland

How often have you implored me, dear friend,[21] to tell you more about my experiences in the North.[22] Any failure by now to meet your full satisfaction on this score lies primarily in my reluctance to drag myself anew through all the details of my past. I also highly doubt that I could fully respond, enough to do justice to your request, since the life, rituals, customs, and attitudes of Northerners are so diametrically different from ours that I must fear you would find some of it exaggerated, yes, perhaps even improbable. Was it any different for me in the beginning, when I was physically dropped into their midst? It took me years to find my way out of my inner astonishment at everything around me and all that I saw and heard.

/[23]The ingenuity of the people here[24] is, in general, quite remarkable. They excel, at any rate, in their mental abilities. And yet, they are also—for our way

---

21 The identity of this female friend is not known, nor even if it was an actual person or various people to whom the author wrote. See the preceding translator's essay "About the Manuscript" on page xx above.
22 The author places Germany, and Europe more broadly, in the North relative to her homeland Zanzibar, as well as her patriarchal country of origin, Oman, in the South, and similarly refers to the Occident relative to the Orient and the West relative to the East.
23 The author's original manuscript featured long, continuous sections, many of which carried over multiple pages. The translator has divided these extended pieces into multiple paragraphs for greater readability, in each case denoted by a "/" to indicate a paragraph or section break added by the translator.
24 "Here" being Germany, where the author lived from 1867 to 1888, after leaving Zanzibar, and then again from 1914 until her death in 1924. See the "Timeline" on pages 153–57 below.

of being—rather too prosaic, so that from our perspective it is hard to get into their mindset. Generally welcoming toward strangers, they especially delight in giving special attention and care to people who are their opposites. By contrast, the imposing reality hits the newcomer with such heft that he cannot, for lack of any understanding, help but seek refuge only in himself. People here may well be shaped by an excess of culture; there is hardly any other explanation. Then, too, this culture seems to breed conceit and, for some, goes hand-in-hand with arrogance. Both are certainly very ugly traits, and such people are best avoided. Overall, this is a place where weaklings will go under if they cannot sufficiently counter the endless moral blows that are seemingly part and parcel of this civilization. How often did I catch myself over time in this less than consoling thought: Are you, truly, awake or asleep?

/But why get ahead of the facts?[25]

---

[25] This "beautiful but elusive" opening passage is perhaps best understood in retrospect, as suggested by my third cousin, Alexander von Brand, who is also descended from Sayyida Salme. He recommends returning to this first section after completing the *Letters*, and optimally also the *Memoirs*. In this way, readers, too, will not "get ahead of the facts," but rather let the account speak for itself in substantiating the author's trenchant introductory observations.

1[26]

Our journey on the Red Sea[27] was indescribably hot. Around midday, no one dared spend time under the awning, and all passengers had to stay in the salon until the sun dipped more to the West. Sitting down to eat with so many completely unknown gentlemen and ladies made me very uncomfortable, and I was always happy when mealtimes came to an end, all the more because I suspected the presence of pork or lard in every dish. I thus passed on anything that I sensed contained pig and instead lived off only biscuits, boiled eggs, tea, and fruit during those early days. My false pride kept me from telling my husband about my fear of these unclean, and for us strictly forbidden, animals, knowing that Christians have no restrictions and make no distinction between "clean" and "unclean." I therefore mostly feigned lack of appetite and put my hope in the future, which so often works wonders.

/If there was anything that seemed to mock my past seclusion from the world of men, then it was these few nights here onboard the ship. Already for several nights now, all first-class passengers—male and female—had been sleeping on their mattresses all together in the salon. I was no fan of this new kind of freedom but, aspiring to be civilized, had to join in. For when I explained to my husband that I would rather sleep in the suffocatingly hot cabin, instead of going up to the salon as he suggested, he turned to a very amiable Madame C.[28] from Mauritius, of French birth. This lady gave me absolutely no rest until she had extracted my firm promise to sleep upstairs together with the other passengers. In recognition of my concession, she promised to sleep by my side the whole time. And the best part was the display the next morning when everyone awoke! The gentlemen all in nightshirts with thin, white night trousers, and nothing more. The ladies all in long English nightgowns under thin, white slips. And of course, no one wore stockings. Indeed, only a few individuals had woolen blankets for cover. As soon as anyone awoke, they immediately made themselves scarce, that no one might see them in their scant attire.

---

26 All subdivisions are included as they appear in the author's original manuscript, except in the few cases preceded by /. The subdivision numeration has been added by the translator for ease of reference.

27 The author took this trip with her new husband, Rudolph Heinrich Ruete (known as Heinrich), who had just rejoined her nine months after she fled Zanzibar. They left Aden, Yemen, on May 30, 1867, and traveled by sea and train to Hamburg, Germany, her husband's city of origin. This short travel description complements the author's "Great Transformations" (*Grosse Wandlungen*) chapter in her *Memoiren einer arabischen Prinzessin* (1886). *Memoirs*, pp. 201–03.

28 As with many of the abbreviated names in the author's account, the identity of this lady is unknown. See the "List of Abbreviations" on page 152.

2

The first European city I ever saw was Marseille. Although we arrived in the month of June, I nonetheless froze to such a degree that dear Madame C. was kind enough to wrap me in her shawl. I possessed no warm clothes of my own, and my outfit was only suited for the Tropics, in no way for the Northern Hemisphere. Thus freezing, we arrived at customs, where the numerous customs officials immediately descended upon our various travel effects. Soon matters became somewhat uncomfortable for my husband, as the gesticulations and loud words of the officials increased, from what I was able to observe from the corner where I sat. Since I could comprehend nothing of what was being said, I pressed my way over to my husband to discover the cause of these exchanges. And so I learned what all the fuss was about. Upon opening our hand luggage, the officials had come upon my Arab jewelry, which they then wanted to tax in the belief that these were commercial goods being imported for sale. Whereupon my husband explained that these were all personal items belonging to his wife and anything but commercial. This was the cause of the dispute, for these dutiful officials had never before, so it seemed, come across the precious jewelry of an Oriental woman. When my husband's assurances that the entire collection belonged to his wife appeared to have no effect, he, too, lost his patience and finally told the officials my birth name. Thus ensued deep bows on the part of the officials, nor could they keep from staring at me with bald curiosity. Enough, my things were finally released to me untaxed, and we could at last make our way to a hotel. Upon arrival, I was so cold, I had to go straight to bed.

/We naturally planned the very next day to look up Madame M.[29] and her niece, whom you of course got to know and love in Zanzibar not all too long ago. Both ladies spoke such good Swahili, and the husband such good Arabic, that it was a true pleasure for me,[30] not to mention that we had so much of the past to talk about. At this time, they lived in the upscale part of Marseille, in a truly lovely villa with a large garden, where they welcomed us with utmost hospitality. On the drive from the hotel to their place, I saw a large house that greatly caught my attention. I inquired about it and learned this was an orphanage, where young children without parents were tended to and cared for until they were old enough to take care of themselves. This straightforward explanation made

---

29 Madame Mass was the wife of Bonaventura Mass. The author first got to know the Spanish couple in Zanzibar and then stayed with them during part of her sojourn in Aden, before re-encountering them in Marseille. E. van Donzel, p. 19; *Memoirs*, p. 202.
30 The author grew up speaking Swahili, the indigenous language of Zanzibar where she lived, and Arabic, the language of the Omani Sultanate into which she was born. Her father, the Sultan, expected the family to speak only Arabic—which was also the language in which the author was taught to read and then secretly taught herself to write—but other languages filled the house when he was not around. *Memoirs*, pp. 26, 36, 55–56.

a huge impression on me, and I found such an institution to be extraordinarily praiseworthy and humane.

/We stayed in beautiful Marseille about a week, and the thought of continuing our travels to northern Germany filled me daily with an ever increasing, totally indescribable trepidation. It was not the climate conditions, which were indeed practically without parallel to ours; no, it was the unknown! At least here in Marseille I had the incredibly dear M. family, who spoke my language and loved my homeland so much. The M. couple, who were originally from Spain, treated us as lovingly as parents would their own children. How comfortable, oh how comfortable they made me feel! The thought of leaving them enveloped me with a melancholy beyond words. Our good friends must have been struck by the same feeling, for when we were ready to reembark on our travels, we received only a letter from them admitting their weakness, that there was simply no way they could take their personal leave of us. Such dear people! Before we left Marseille, Madame M. had pulled together a small trousseau of clothes for me, suited for the Northern clime, at my husband's request.

As we drove from our hotel to the train station, I was gripped by such an unfamiliar fear that I would have preferred to scream out loud. I had the feeling as though, from this moment on, my homeland was being pulled ever further from me, and all the bridges were crashing in behind me. The cry of my soul for you turned into a thousand voices from my beloved island, all seemingly calling to me in unison: "Do not go any further, better to return again!" I fought a terrible fight within myself. Like an automaton, I stepped into the train that would now seek to take me, as quickly as possible, to an unknown land, to total strangers, as if I was in the greatest hurry to reach my future destination. And so we kept on riding toward the North.

It was an afternoon, just as the sun was going down, that we arrived in Hamburg, my husband's hometown. As a carriage took us through the busy streets, my husband called to me and pointed to a person passing by, wearing very short sleeves and a white cap on the head. She seemed to be carrying something bulky under her arm, which she kept covered with a cloth. "Did you see that person, Bibi?"[31] he asked. Then he explained that this was a servant girl, wearing the same outfit as virtually all servant girls in Hamburg. Until now, I had never seen so many fair-skinned and blond people, which naturally struck me as very odd, and the same with the long strides and hurried pace that practically everyone on the street seemed to have.

---

31 "Bibi" can mean wife in Swahili and is also associated with *habibi* meaning "my love" in Arabic, as a term of both endearment and high respect (see also Bibi Azze, the author's stepmother and Sultan's principal wife in the *Memoirs*, p. 8).

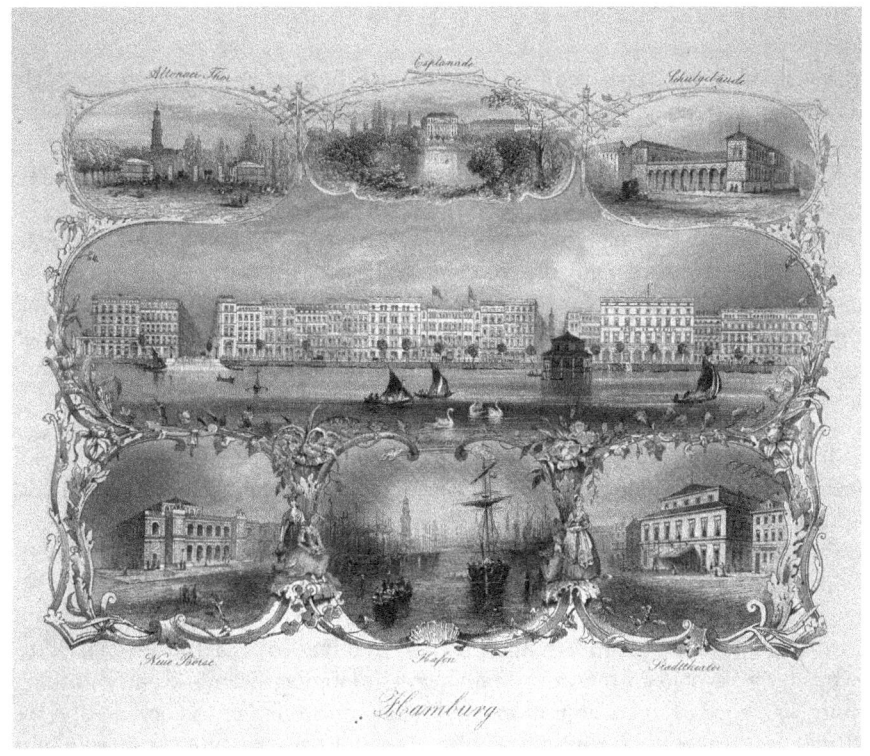

Steel engraving of Hamburg, mid-1800s.

3

You will, of course, also want to know what I thought and felt in those early days on European soil, am I right? Yes, I was wholly and completely overcome by the strangest of sensations. All in all—and I admit this freely—I constantly felt anxious, and it was only in the presence of my husband that I could free myself from this excruciating feeling that tormented me both day and night. Everything was so foreign, so very different, from what I had known and been accustomed to before. Only one voice still rang out within my soul—since I was unable to comprehend anything else—as it pitched a constant refrain: "And this is where you want to spend the rest of your days?"[32] I would have sooner given up my life before I could have answered this horrid question with an honest "yes."

/On top of that, to be called Christian, even though I was as much a Muslim inside as you yourself. Through and through, I felt so despicable that I should appear different from what I actually was. I will tell you this in unvarnished frankness: Beware of changing your religion without complete conviction! Conviction? Yes, from whom and what should I have gained any conviction? No one, as it was, cared one whit about my true faith.[33] It was apparently enough for the pastor at my baptism and ensuing wedding to hear me say "yes"[34] to everything he said to me in a totally foreign language, since clearly nothing more was needed. As of that moment, I had been won over to Christianity; for all the rest, I would be on my own. Back then, I truly knew little more about being a Christian than you. And the consequences did not fail to take their course.

/Divorced from my old beliefs, and attached to the new in name only, I began a time for which I have no words. Never in my whole life—neither before nor after—did I feel so morally bereft, robbed of every support, as right after my

---

32 The final typewritten manuscript inserts a handwritten superscript number 1 at this point, signaling a possible footnote. Similar superscripts appear throughout this manuscript at several dozen locations, especially next to abbreviated names. These superscripts are not part of the original handwritten manuscript and were all added posthumously. Unfortunately, the intended contents of any footnotes have been lost to time, and the markings have accordingly been omitted here.

33 The original handwritten manuscript contains an insertion labeled "10A" here, with content that does not fit the narration. Since the pagination at this point also jumps from page 5 to page 11, something appears to have gone awry, and some text may have gotten lost. Insertion 10A reads: "Here I made my first acquaintance with the so very superfluous gloves (except in winter). I could not fathom their utility, considering as well that the eager salesman in the store took, as it seemed to me, all too much time and effort with my hands."

34 The word "yes" appears in the handwritten German original, meaning the author responded to the pastor with her wedding vows in English.

baptism. Had you been witness to my inner struggles back then, that would have sufficed for you to soften your stances against me. My expectation that *every* follower of Christ would take me, lead me, and guide me in matters of the Lord, to induct me into religious ways and thus build my inner faith as one of them, unfortunately proved a complete deception. Soon I also came to see the power of religion as the most powerful of all when it comes to affecting our inner lives and well-being. I felt so despicably false to be considered a Christian when I had absolutely no clear idea *how and what* Christianity even means. I knew only what stood in the Koran, nothing more. As for my inner peace, it would have been far better had I at least stayed true to my old faith at the start. For there is no doubt that it is a thousand times better to be a Muslim than to be neither Christian (meaning from the heart) nor Muslim. And it was with this largest possible chasm inside me that I entered Europe and its hallowed civilization. I fought internally with myself, no one surmising how much I suffered in silence. Not even to my own beloved husband could I openly admit that our views differed on this point.

Oh, I will never ever forget the day during our short stopover in Cairo on our way to Europe. Here we visited the famous Muhammad Ali Mosque on the Citadel, where we had to pull felt slippers over our shoes before entering. I was unaware of what this requirement meant, but then found out that entry into the mosque without overshoes is strictly forbidden of all non-Muslims. This is when I realized what I had in fact become. In my eyes, there is no greater sacrifice than changing religion; neither rank, riches, nor the highest worldly status can feel as irreplaceable to us as our sacred faith. To console you, I can also let you know that, in the initial years after my baptism, I instinctively recited my old prayer to myself whenever I was alone.

Soon I drew inward and became reticent, and always deflected my husband's anxious questions if something was wrong by simply pretending homesickness. Why discuss something when the views are so diametric? When we are younger, we can hardly imagine how much people stay attached to their upbringings throughout their lifetimes, no matter how much the circumstances may change over time.

4

I lived through this initial period in Europe as in a dream. Instead of two eyes and two ears, I wished for ten of each to take in all the new and incredible things around me. The wildest fantasies a person could ever invent and imagine will suddenly and abruptly confront you here all at once. Although I am no weakling by nature, I felt on edge in a way I could not shake. In a word, it was almost eerie. Everything, but everything is different here: houses, streets, clothes, food—yes, even the air and the people! There was no end to what I had to absorb and process all at once. With all the languages, manners, and customs completely foreign to me, my position was hardly optimal, all the more because immediately upon arriving in Hamburg, we had to go straight into the obligatory round of visits to my husband's family and friends. Nothing is more dreadful than the so-called courtesy calls that they do here. And then to have the bad luck of being Arab—not speaking a word of German. No, I was close to despair.—The physiognomy of the people, with names that were impossible for me to pronounce, speaking a language I could not remotely understand, full of sounds like s, sch, t, tz, that were practically lively bird twitter to my ears, left me very confused. No wonder that I almost felt bewitched.

/One curious trait struck me right from the start, namely the way these people perpetually smile. It matters not what time of day you might show up, your host will always be smiling, except of course when you come to convey condolences. Privately, I referred to the Germans as simply a "happy nation," but my husband soon set me straight. This perpetual smiling, he told me, was in no way to be taken at face value; it was just customary good manners, with no particular meaning. Some may have a rather cheerful mien, but both inside and in reality, they are anything but cheerful. You can surely imagine how surprised I was by this. Your natural demeanor would not be all too well-received here, and rather than the customary cloth mask, which is not the norm here, you would have to sport a natural mask, as much as your facial muscles would allow. There is no point in protesting against such ingrained habits, since sooner or later, you must succumb to the usual practice. These and similar things are resolutely required and demanded by this exacting dame that we call Civilization.

/I also have to share with you the masterful way people are able to shape their thoughts and speech here. Oh, there is so much to learn in this place, an endless amount. At first, it all felt so strange. To be exclusively around white people, and so many with blond hair! It took a long time before I got used to that. I even found it hard to distinguish people from each other; to my unpracticed eye, they all looked so very much alike. My greatest difficulty, however, lay in the often totally unpronounceable names of the locals. Once I managed to get over that hurdle, I then often ran into issues with the customary forms of address. Despite endless explanations, I could not initially grasp the difference between the words "Sie" and "Du," so that I often enough mixed them up, saying "Du" to strangers and "Sie" to my husband's relatives. Meanwhile, I would catch the bemused smiles of strangers, notably the gentlemen, which soon prompted me to pay more attention to my use of "Sie" and "Du." My inability to speak a single European language, in particular German, took such a major toll on me early on that I resolved I would not rest until I had learned the native tongue.

/Just imagine you are situated in a household without being able to speak to your servants. You must pay visits to strangers and your entire conversations consist exclusively of handshakes. The same thing repeats when they undertake the unavoidable return visits to you. You are invited to a large social gathering, where all eyes are on you, whose gazes reveal nothing but nosiness. Ladies and gentlemen stare at you from head to foot for so long that you, as a matter of decorum, are forced to lower your astonished eyes. You need something and would like to have it, but there is no way to obtain it without your husband nearby, since he must translate all your occasional wishes and needs to the servants. Every day, except Sunday, I was completely unable to speak and remained consistently mute from nine-thirty to four while my husband was in his office. All this, as you can see, was of more than trivial consequence for me. And so I had no alternative but to learn the local language.

/With life made so unbearable, I promised myself, as mentioned, to put all my energy into learning this language, indeed for two reasons: first, to address the helplessness of my situation, as I have described, and second, for fear of you at home, knowing that people here could easily interpret my personal incompetence as generally characteristic of "Arabs." I was determined to do all I could to learn the customs and habits of the land where I now lived as quickly as possible, in order to keep what many perceived as our primitive upbringing from also being stamped an object of general pity.

/Upon my inquiry, my husband engaged an expert lady, who spent every afternoon from one to three teaching me, with admirable patience, first the names of household items and then reading and writing. Truly, it must have been more than boring for my teacher back then to wander with me from room to room, even down to the basement kitchen and up to the attic, to show me individual objects that were unfamiliar to me, but also could not be readily brought to me.

/I also had great difficulty with writing at the time. Instead of writing from right to left as before, I now needed to take my pen from left to right. It also took some time for me to understand why there were big and small letters. Of course, I had to learn the ABC's just like a five-year-old child. Except for a few letters, such as Ö, Ü, Ä, I fortunately soon knew these basic building blocks by heart. After eleven months of tutoring, I could even dare to join in with a word here or there. From this point on, it did not take long before I was able to keep the household book myself, understandably to the annoyance of our, until then, self-governing servants. What is a household book? Something that you naturally do not even know by name. Whereas in your home, you are used to depositing your annual income into a cashbox, counted of course, while your expenditures are then taken out again uncounted, matters here are handled altogether differently. The assets and liabilities of every individual play a much greater role than you might at first be able to comprehend.

/In the practical ways of the North, everything is done systematically, and the sense of order is admirable. Precise accounting is expected from everyone across the board, and woe to anyone who carries on mindlessly into the day. Even the Ministers, the actual government of every country, must account for every penny they spend to maintain the whole. Children toward their parents and wives to their husbands must answer for the funds they receive, if so requested. When young children start going to school, even they are taught this method with the allowances they get, so they can later maintain their own households. As you can see, this place is based on such an excellent system that it can only be praised. People here are raised with a feeling of responsibility, and this aspect of society cannot be overly appreciated. Motivated by what I observed from others, I, too, as mentioned, soon started to maintain our household accounts and write up all our expenditures.

5 House[35]

Having arrived in Hamburg mid-summer, we moved into a little villa on the beautiful Alster, with the later intention of buying a small house. From the start, I thoroughly disliked the tiny rooms that are typical of the houses here, whose narrow and low-ceilinged spaces were so cramped and anxiety-inducing. I was always relieved when I could breathe in the fresh and free air. People, it seems to me, care more about the number of rooms than their size. Space in the rooms is even further constrained by placing useful and useless furniture right in the middle and in all the corners, often making it difficult to navigate between all the "essential" items. Here, doors to the rooms are even kept shut by day, something that very much struck me, since I had never encountered that before. It took a long time before I could get used to this rather uncomfortable necessity. Outside doors to the houses are also closed the whole day, for there are no doormen to keep watch day and night as with us, except in hotels.

/You have absolutely no idea what all it takes to furnish a European household. As we were setting up our living quarters, there was no end to the incoming stream of hundreds of things. I was above all astonished by the sight of the vast quantities of kitchen utensils that are required here. I could not help but think of the mass feedings in our house, where at least ten kinds of baked goods and other kinds of sweets had to be prepared daily, and yet it was all done with so few instruments.

/The tight and disquieting feeling in our house was accentuated even more by the sight of thick, ribbed curtains, which threatened to obscure my view of the beloved sun, whose appearance was already so limited. Having to sit exclusively on chairs left me quite miserable in the beginning, and I harbored no small jealousy toward your comfortable "meddes" and "tekjes"! (The former being a kind of low, very soft divan; the latter, padded cushions about three feet square.) But outfitted with corset and crinoline, as I now was, and feeling caught in a vise the whole long day, I would have been very challenged to sit on a medde.

In the beginning, too, I was extremely loathe to bathe in a bathtub, but even this, as with so much else, was something I had to get used to over time. It seemed so unclean to have to wash our bodies in stagnant water, instead of what we were accustomed to at home. In response to my question as to why the same

---

35 This is the only subdivision title provided by the author. All subdivision headers provided by Heinz Schneppen in his publication of the original German are, as he noted, not part of the author's original manuscript, including a modified version of this header. H. Schneppen, *Briefe*, p. 9.

simple drain arrangement was not possible here, I was told the climate was too cold. I very much liked how the water pipes and gas lighting were set up. The degree to which European households maintain order and keep things clean is exemplary and even quite exaggerated in some of the houses.

/People are generally not very enamored of bathing, even though it is, in my opinion, far more essential than keeping the floors clean. Young children are bathed daily only up to a certain age, and thereafter only once a week. For older ages, it is best not to ask. When T.[36] was born, she was given a nanny who seriously needed a bath, something we had to tell her before we could entrust her with the child. It was not easy to persuade this genuine farm woman to undergo the salubrious act. Only after a lengthy back-and-forth did she begrudgingly step into the tub.

/Among other things, we purchased an English four-poster canopy bed, which we both liked very much and whose size reminded me of our Indian-style beds. But how can I describe my surprise when the bed was all made up with its heavy curtains, and inside lay two massive feather beds. When I asked what was the meaning of these monstrosities—up to this point, I had seen only quilts and flannel blankets - I was informed of their indispensable nature. Nevertheless, in the lowliness of my uncivilized state, I considered it a major imposition to have to cover myself with these appalling chicken feathers (as was translated to me at the time), and I refused.

The food here, I felt, was cooked much too blandly, and early on, it was quite hard for me to get used to what was served. Most of all, the thought of pork simply horrified me. It took me forever, and only after extensive cajoling, before I could agree to eat the meat of these less than appetizing creatures. Cooking, an activity where we, as children, used to bring our resident kitchen staff to despair, served me very well here. At times when I could not bring myself to consume what we would have considered just a bunch of trifles, I simply went into the kitchen and cooked myself some curry and pilaf. Anything else would have needed tools that were lacking and mostly do not exist here. The first time I got sick and lost my appetite, the doctor recommended that I eat oysters. Of course, I did not understand what he said at the time, but when my husband translated the word into Swahili, I was indignant.[37] As you know, none of us eats oysters back home, except possibly the absolute wildest native Africans.

---

36 This refers to the author's eldest daughter Tony, who was born Antonie (Arabic "Thawka") Ruete on March 24, 1868.
37 Swahili was the common language between the author and her husband, who had learned the language as a German merchant trading on the island of Zanzibar, where they met. (*Memoirs*, pp. 201–03).

That early period was truly terrible for me, especially after the contract with the English woman we had brought with us came to an end, and she accordingly had to return to her husband. I spoke Hindustani[38] with her and could converse some while my husband was away, usually from nine-thirty to four. And so it was that, after she left for England, I barely spoke a word for seven, pensive hours of every day. I had absolutely nothing to do, of course, nor anything to read, since I had already read all the Arab books my husband had ordered for me from Alexandria at least ten times over and knew them practically by heart. I did not yet know how to do European needlework, and so I found secret joy, crazy as it may seem, in welcoming every new hole in our stockings that I could set about darning. And yet, this peculiar pleasure occurred only rarely, since I had but recently forced my freedom-loving feet into stockings and owned only new ones.

To kill some time in these lonely hours, when I was quite literally speechless, my Arab articles of jewelry and clothing were imposed upon. With them, I could silently share my thoughts, no words needed. Were these not the only items I had to remind me of you and my beloved homeland? As childish as it may sound, I openly admit that I sometimes hugged and kissed these lifeless things during this exercise, but only behind closed doors. Quite often my husband would enter when the whole room was still strewn about with unpacked items and would then help me pack them up again. Now—upon seeing my husband and my familiar things all around me—I could again dare to doubt the power of sorcery, even though a belief in real bewitching so often crept over me.

---

38 Hindustani, a hybridized lingua franca derived primarily from Hindi and Urdu, was the language of "Hindustan," the Persian variant for Land of the Indus, or northern India (including what is now Pakistan). Zanzibar drew many traders, financiers, artisans, and others, along with their families, from the area.

/You will consider it ridiculous that I, who as a child was the wildest among you, without any trepidation or terror, would become so anxious in this new environment, in a way you can hardly imagine. Every time my husband left the house to go to his office, I would tremble with fear. My dread would fill me and shatter my nerves so much that I would often burst into tears. In a word, it felt beyond petrifying to have to exist in the midst of all that was so new.

/No wonder then that I would await my husband's arrival every day already starting at three in the afternoon, when I knew full well that he could not come before four. He rarely arrived with empty pockets, which he usually took care to fill with southern fruits. One day he brought me fresh pomegranates. I took one look and could not hold back the tears, as these were the first I had seen in Europe, with all the many old memories they evoked.

My first "white" cook was called Lene, and I naturally did my best to communicate with her through pantomime. One day, on a Sunday when my husband's relatives usually came over for lunch, I was headed to the basement to get something when I came across our worthy Lene as she was preparing the coffee. I personally stayed away from this wonderful drink for more than two years after my arrival in Europe for the simple reason that what people here call coffee does not even begin to deserve the label. But had I indulged in European coffee at the time of this incident, it would have undoubtedly killed my appetite for coffee henceforth. Namely, there she stood, diligently dripping coffee through an old stocking. In response to my gesticulated query about how she could possibly do such a thing, she came back with a naïve enough answer: "But Madam, the stockings are of course freshly washed!" Straight to the point, I took the instrument out of her hand and threw it into the fire.

/When we first moved into the house, I asked my husband how many cooks we would actually need, which made him burst out at me in hearty laughter. He then replied, to my great consternation, that Europeans, even very rich ones, tended to keep only one cook per household. Of course, I was thinking of our conditions back home, where people take the slightest opportunity to say they are sick, causing us to always have a second and sometimes even third person available to step in. But I also realized soon enough that a stout German maidservant could achieve ten times more than a native African.

The unusually long summer days made a big impression on me here, since every day for you has only twelve hours, regardless if summer or winter. How good of Mother Nature to have so wisely arranged this time frame to suit practicing Muslims with their annual, sun-up to sundown, thirty days of continuous fasting, during which any kind of food or drink is prohibited, as opposed to destining the residents of Greenland or Siberia to these daytime restrictions.

6

The consequence of our visits was unavoidable; we were in turn courteously invited back by all. Hamburg dinner parties are famous far and wide in Germany, and that is justified, as no one prizes a well-appointed table as much as here. For my part, these dinners were simply excruciating. Seeing as how I usually had the honor of being led by the gentlemen of the house to the table, they apparently also took it as their personal duty to fill my plate with delicacies and encourage me to eat them all. It is also not uncommon to stay seated from six to ten, a full four hours by the clock, with ten to twelve glasses arrayed at one's place. Added to that, people are so loud and talkative that my head would often spin. For certain, all this talk at mealtimes is a European peculiarity that we Arabs do not share.

/Because grace is very rarely said at mealtimes in Germany, everyone apparently has to take care of thanking the Giver of all earthly things in private. At least so I thought at the time, until I was informed that this was simply not customary. Table prayers are not said even in the closest family circles, or at most only among the very devout. Of course, this was completely alien to me, since I had up to that point assumed that all people, whether pious or not, rich or poor, high or low, owe thanks for their existence and well-being, yes, in fact, for everything, entirely to the good Lord.

My untrained eye often took great offense at the deep décolletés of the ladies. And truly, it makes no sense to me even to this day why one would choose to expose so much to hundreds of individuals of both sexes, when on other occasions that appear much less consequential, one is then demure. Even so, it is rather peculiar that people feel less shame when they see a native African woman, who often wears only an animal-hide apron, than when they see a white lady in her low-cut dress.

The first ball, where I went as an observer, had a very strange effect on me, for the many people and all their incessant swirling actually made me dizzy. As I watched the way people engaged in animated conversation and saw the gentlemen lead the ladies with their demonstrative low cuts to the dance floor, it was obvious to me that long years of friendship had created close and intertwined bonds among all who were assembled here. But I was then informed, no matter how unbelievable it sounded to me, that many on the dance floor had met and spoken here for the very first time! That is when I really grasped the extent to which I was still a stranger here. People also frequently asked me on those occasions whether we, too, danced back home. When I explained that we did not dance ourselves, but instead let others dance for us, people considered this all too droll.

Heinrich Ruete, the author's husband

The author, likely around 1868.

Invitations often arrived four weeks in advance, which left plenty of time to live and die in the meantime. The idea that people would stay at a party so late into the night, thereby getting to bed only at three or four in the morning, was new to me. I was always happy when we were finally headed back home again. Since there were so few exotic individuals to be seen in Germany at the time—relative to England and France—I suffered immensely during those first years. At parties, in theatres and concerts, I felt like I was under constant surveillance, which I found extremely vexing. My husband and I were taking a walk one day when some ladies drove by in a carriage. It was not enough for them to blatantly stare at us as they passed, but when I happened to turn around, I saw them both kneeling on the back seat to get a closer look. I later learned these ladies belonged to Hamburg's "high-life." Through experiences like this, I became so reluctant to be among people that I almost always rode in a closed carriage and turned down invitations whenever I could.

/Having usually worn the full rainbow of colors, I found European outfits all too dreary. Tastes have, however, shifted considerably over the past few years. In some circles where people are wedded to fashion, they now simply seek to outdo the Orientals. I was especially struck by all the little children whose totally white outfits made them look like ghosts, as compared to our children, who are already clothed in bright clothing from birth.

With regard to the theory of "human equality" that is so widely extolled by its proponents in the North, I had a very tangible experience. One day we were walking along a relatively narrow street. A servant girl carrying a large handbasket was coming in our direction, but rather than move to the side, she chose to bump into me with her basket, thus causing considerable damage to my new, pearl-decorated, silken mantilla. So this, I thought to myself, is a demonstrative test by a republican[39] servant girl in the push for freedom. This type of person, by which I mean European servants, as hard-working and useful as they are, often behaves so boldly and brashly that I was at times tempted to stroke their characteristically red cheeks in a less than delicate manner. But my husband let me know that a slap in the face is subject to a ten thaler penalty. I naturally preferred to withhold my ten thalers from both the police and the obstinate girl in question, and instead behave, as much as possible, in a "civilized" fashion.

/People already had more than enough outlandish tales to tell about the Arab lady. To wit, I was as fat as a barrel, even though at the time I looked more like a

---

39 "Republican" here refers to someone favoring a republic form of German government, in contrast to a royalist.

beanpole. I had the hair and complexion of a native black African. My feet were as small as those of a Chinese woman, which naturally meant I could not walk. These good folk probably had no idea that this purported Chinese woman went on walking tours from Reinbeck to Bergedorf and all around the Alster.[40] I still remember when a gentleman acquaintance came to visit us for the first time, how he could not hide his surprise at finding me as the Lord had made me, rather than the product of all these fantasies. My husband was often enough at pains to make the simple-minded Northerners understand that there is a big difference between Arabs and native Africans, and that other peoples besides native Africans also lived in greater Africa. I even had to put up with a very naïve lady who engrossed herself in my supposedly African hair and then took the strange liberty of touching it! This was but the second time I had met her.

I cannot describe how I froze that first summer, and in July and August, I was often seen moving about the house wrapped in a flannel blanket. One of my pleasures was working in the garden and watering the lawn with the rubber hose. The pretty white cat, which cousin H. had brought to Zanzibar from Mecca and later gave to me—the one that made you so jealous—was unfortunately stolen from us here. This loss made me very sad, for she was a living emblem of the homeland and very dear to me. As a replacement, my husband soon gave me two pet dogs, a poodle and a greyhound, who often reminded me of your ingrained aversion to these very devoted creatures. I also received a singing canary and a milk-bearing goat, and so I found my daily joy in this little menagerie. The same way we used to love to milk the cows and goats on the plantations, to the dismay of our female attendants, I now also milked our goat with my own hands.

The environment around Hamburg is absolutely delightful, especially the area along the Elbe, where I always loved to go. We accordingly spent the entire Sunday there virtually every second or third week. I had a very special fondness for the port, where I saw the ships that sailed to you, and now and again Africans that come here as sailors. How very comical they looked in their European clothes, and the poor souls usually appeared to be frozen and miserable.

I often experienced the downsides of not knowing the native language. Here is a funny example of one such trial: One day, I lost my way downtown and could not figure out how to get back. By chance, I happened upon the street where our shoemaker lives. I went in and could do no better than the English phrase: show me. Whereupon the shoemaker had nothing more urgent to do than to

---

40 Distances of approximately five kilometers and seven and a half kilometers, respectively.

pull up a chair for me, grab my foot, and start to take measurements to fit a pair of boots. Astonished by this act, I wrested my foot from between his hands. Totally baffled, he went out and got someone who better understood my "show me" and pointed me in the right direction. The good man had taken the English words to indicate a desire for a pair of shoes.

The need to always close the door upon entering or leaving a room or other space—even the house door, which for you only happens at night—made no sense to me. I habitually left the doors open, even in the winter. I also could not fathom why, despite rooms that were usually so small, and then even in the summer, doors and windows had to be kept shut. Accustomed to living with open windows, year in, year out, day and night, I initially did not do well with the used-up air that was so offensive to the nose. Any time I found myself in a room with too little ventilation, I got a headache. Just consider how my love of fresh air unwittingly made me the laughingstock of the neighborhood, only because I frequently opened the windows for long periods even in the winter. The word was that I was also heating the streets.

7

The first snow I ever saw struck me as simply too bizarre. Even today, I can recall the exact hour that I watched the first flakes swirl down from the sky. I sat as usual, idle and alone, in the anteroom awaiting my husband's return from the city. The lonelier I felt in my new surroundings, the quicker my thoughts rushed to you, so that, in effect, I was living two lives: one in my mind, bathed in the eternal blue sky and teeming with all your dear figures, full of high spirits and mischief; the other in the reality of my destiny. It appeared all too odd to me that anyone up in the sky would try to spread lots of white wadding onto this dirty earth, a rather pointless exercise it seemed, since at first the flakes simply would not stay on the ground. At that moment, I could not yet explain this display and instead became uncomfortable. I awaited my husband's return with even more impatience than usual, so that he would solve this Northern puzzle for me.

/This was also the time that my dear husband, in his concern for my well-being, could not dress me warmly enough. I was very displeased by all this, since I thoroughly disliked how much attire the rough climate here requires. You cannot imagine what all I had to layer on, all at the same time. Not infrequently, my dear husband would come rushing after me with some item of clothing in his hands, calling: *Bibi! Wewe umasahaw[41] kitu!* (My wife, you have forgotten something.) To which my response was always the same: *Siku sahaw lakini sipendi.* (I have not forgotten anything; I just do not like it.)

/I found it awful when I was supposed to wrap a heavy scarf around my neck; it felt like someone wanted to choke me. I also soon realized that people can rarely afford to leave the house without an umbrella. Men, women, and children head out day and night armed with this completely indispensable item, which at first sight would also very likely make you suspect some danger in the vicinity. Is that not so? Very different from how it is for us at home, where people live and die without ever having called a single umbrella their own. Actually, the Northern winter is one of

---

41 The last letter of this Swahili word is unclear in the typewritten original (Leiden University Libraries Or. 6281), but the author's handwritten original clearly shows a "w" at the end of "umasaha-" (Or. 27.135 A3). More generally, the Swahili phrases in this translation are shown as they appear in the author's manuscripts, while her German translations of the Swahili have been replaced with English translations. Professor van Donzel has footnoted alternate Swahili spellings, perhaps to clarify meanings or make corrections, citing to G.S.P. Freeman-Grenville's heavily-researched and well-annotated edition of *Memoirs of an Arabian Princess* from 1981. Nevertheless, the author's spellings may reflect the local Zanzibari dialect of her time and may also represent a more phonetic transliteration, since the author learned as a native without being schooled in Swahili.

the greatest wonders of the world, to the unending astonishment of the Tropics. Can you believe that people and creatures all start steaming when the temperature reaches certain levels in the winter? How amazed I was to see the horses on the street letting off steam at the same time I saw so much steam coming out of my own mouth.

/Once on a winter drive in a closed carriage, I saw through the glass pane how the coachman repeatedly pounded his chest with both arms. Alarmed by this remarkable demonstration, my first thought was that the poor man had suddenly lost his senses. I naturally wanted to leave the carriage as quickly as possible, but my husband broke out in hearty laughter and tried to calm me, while also explaining that the poor coachman needed this motion to keep himself warm. Did you ever consider—not in a dream, but in real life—that one could cross a river, on foot or in a heavy coach, without getting even the slightest bit wet? Indeed, this is an annual spectacle under conditions that often last two to three months here. You can shake your head as much as you want, it is simply so. In light of all these odd occurrences, which I would have considered completely out of the question only a short time before, should I not have believed this to be some kind of magic?

Two instruments, called barometer and thermometer, are of great importance here. People frequently look to the first one with avid anticipation because its readings rather often determine the dispositions of individuals, although with no impact on their moods. The second one by contrast, to the extent it is found in a closed room, registers very randomly in the winter. With some people it is high, with others it is low, such that I, too, soon started paying attention to this house friend and advisor. Oh, across the board, I never, ever seemed to get out of learning mode, for the list of things to learn here can hardly be enumerated. What little children are able to absorb and learn slowly and successively over time, from the crib onward, all came crowding quickly and completely unmediated into my poor brain, so that I, as I said, could not get past learning.

The onset of this dreary winter also ushers in the so-called social season. For a good six months, people are stuck in their four walls, while the period for sitting outdoors, as in the summer when trees and bushes beguile the hearts and eyes, belongs to the past. Thus begins a time when countless folks, the ones who find cozy familial togetherness much too boring, embark on an existence that is not unlike a frenzied hunt. Such people apparently cannot be happy without, for example, spending the day with A. at breakfast, B. for lunch, and C. for dinner. I personally knew a very sickly lady, who spent most of the day in bed, but just "had" to go out in the evening. Of course, as happened every time, whenever she had to go out, as she herself put it, she would down several glasses of champagne shortly before leaving the house to sustain her weak health. On such occasions, the poor stomach is often subjected to much too much excess. But no harm done when there is still ample socializing and fun to be had, since that is why people simply head to Karlsbad[42] the following spring. It is astounding how little sleep people need to survive here during winter nights; certainly, another triumph of civilization.

Every once in a while, we would also go to the Circus Renz, where I took great delight in the magnificent horses. I was very interested in all the feats the animals performed there. But I was less enamored of the wonderful appearance of the ladies, who seemed to come up short with their attire. What people referred to as outfits in this case were in fact hardly worthy of the name. It was also beyond me how people could enjoy and even cheer for the often quite insipid pantomimes.

/Although I as yet had not the slightest sense for European music, the plan was for me to attend a major concert. For this purpose, I was advised to throw on my red shawl entwined with gold, which, you may recall, was a present from my dear brother M.[43] from his East India trip, and let it hang like a burnoose. But oh, how I regretted that act, for we had hardly entered the great concert hall overflowing with people, when all eyes and opera glasses turned to my unfortunate person. I had no idea that this shawl would serve as a billboard, or I never in my life would have worn it across my shoulders. You can surely imagine how glad I was to finally leave.

After a while, I was told it would also be good if I visited a theatre. "Theatre," I asked my husband, "what is that?" "Yes," he answered, "the theatre is a large house where various plays are performed. Today, for example," he continued, "there is a play that will remind you of your homeland. It is called: The African Woman."[44] We drove there—I was full of anticipation. The commotion from the many people rushing about the theatre brought forth uncomfortable memories of the concert evening with my red burnoose, so I hesitated somewhat going in, especially because I had followed my husband's request and again put on something Oriental, namely a loose jacket with gold embroidery. So that I could see everything better, we took parquet seats near the orchestra. Never in my

---

42 Now Karlovy Vary in the Czech Republic, a renowned spa town with an abundance of large and small hot springs.
43 Possibly the author's half-brother Madjid, who became Sultan of Zanzibar upon their father's death and reigned from 1856 until 1870.
44 "L'Africaine," by Giacomo Meyerbeer (1791–1864), a popular French grand opera that debuted in 1865.

life had I sat so close to European instrumental music, and my unmusical head was battered about quite badly that evening.

/Finally, the curtain was raised, and I now had a very good view of the actors. Since I could not understand a single word of what was being said, I was left to observe the fantastical outfits and rather expressive gestures of the players. Everything seemed so new and peculiar, but hardly natural, and I had next to no sense of the whole thing. When my husband asked if I was enjoying the play, I could only answer "no." I then asked him whether the players were—crazy. "Oh, not at all," he laughingly responded. "But then why are they acting like it, if they are not supposed to be crazy?" was my totally uneducated question. "Of course, this is how the people want to imitate life in Africa." And what was I to say in response to that? Nothing at all!

/Africa is well-known to be very large, but the European imagination seemed to me larger yet. The late Meyerbeer was perhaps happily spared the experience during his lifetime of having such a real African woman in the audience of his play with, as it were, so little appreciation for his art. Most certainly his spirit looked down with great disappointment upon my lack of refinement, and he would have found it even less edifying to see me head home already at nine o' clock. After this first foray into the House of Thalia, there was, predictably for me, little hope that I would fill in my lacking knowledge, despite the considerable subsequent encouragement.

/These theatre performances have nowhere near the effect on Orientals that they have on Europeans; we are apparently missing the necessary understanding for the so widely-admired artistic achievements here. As an example: I later spoke with an Arab, who had also been in a European theatre. I asked: "What did you like the most about the piece you saw?" To which he responded so naturally and simply: "The sunset, Bibi, for it looked exactly the same as in Zanzibar!" My unrefined taste for theatre performances changed little over time; quite so, when I saw in some piece how priests were so disrespectfully satirized. When my neighbor noticed my displeasure, she said totally laconically: "But you are Protestant, are you not? What do you care about Catholic priests?" My only retort was to ask if Catholic priests were not "servants of God" just as much as any Protestant pastor. In my humble opinion, basically anything having to do with religion is a very poor fit for the stage, and that is especially true when presented as caricature. Given the nascent state of my Christianity, what I saw and heard was so disheartening that I went home more aggrieved than pleased.

/The thought that kept me so preoccupied put my poor soul into great conflict. I found so few good examples of devout Christians that I personally felt I was neither fish nor fowl. Separated from my former beliefs, I had nonetheless found no real replacement. How was I, as a Mohammedan, supposed to feel attracted to the new faith, when even the people who were born and bred Christian were so disdainful toward their own religion? Your kind heart would certainly have suffered, had you been able to see into my tormented soul. I judiciously wrote nothing of it. Not even my dearest beloved Ch.[45] was privy to this sore subject. I knew, of course, that she would only repeat her urgent plea that I return as one of yours to the old homeland. More on this later.

---

45 The author's half-sister Chole, who features prominently in the *Memoirs*.

8

After we had made the rounds on all the numerous invitations to dinners, lunches, and suppers, the time came for us to return the favor. That was a hefty shock for me, as this meant I would, for the first time in my domesticity, have to play the hostess for a large gathering. What this job entails, you have no idea. The gathering was expedited through an occurrence that at the time helped me get through the lonely hours. It so happened that two weeks before we decided to undertake the soiree, a mighty tortoise reached us on a sailing ship directly from Zanzibar. The tortoise took up residence in the bathtub, although we used the latter multiple times a week. It was a lot of work for the servants to heave the big beast out and back in every time. I could sit in the bathroom by the tortoise for hours on end, and my thoughts would be hundreds and hundreds of miles from the place where fate had driven us both out—the tortoise and me. And the most nostalgic thoughts would then course through my soul upon seeing the animal sit so still and motionless in the water. I had the illusion that my silent companion must have divined and understood my thoughts and feelings. Ever since the animal's arrival, I had been feeling less lonely and was therefore very saddened when she ultimately, unequivocally, had to be killed. Her meat was namely destined for the mock turtle soup.[46]

---

46 The original manuscript says "Mock-Turtle-Suppe," although technically this was to be real turtle (i.e., tortoise) soup.

For this purpose, we also brought on board a special female cook and two hired servants in tails. Starting early in the morning, I would run up and down the stairs the entire day to supervise our supporting cast, which had since grown to six heads, and lend a direct hand where I thought necessary. In the kitchen, I helped with cleaning the vegetables, drying off plates and glasses, and setting the table for the hired servants in the afternoon. Since some of our expected guests had also been in the South, I prepared an extra curry for them, to the astonishment of my cook, who, it seemed to me, found this unfamiliar dish rather too spicy.

/An indescribable anxiety took hold of me as the time for the guests to arrive came closer. I was absolutely convinced I would be subjected to the utmost criticism and thus sought to put forward whatever I could manage, so as not to suffer a fiasco right from the start. A most apropos saying now came to mind, which translates roughly like this: "If you open your door, then behave accordingly, with dignity; otherwise close your door and hide yourself." And so I thought to myself: Well, if the criticism that will surely come is directed only at me, that would not be so bad; but people may go further and take my own incompetence as a reflection of the ineptness of our race. This worry plagued me the most, as I considered how easily I could botch European manners and customs, without the faintest notion of having done so. At that moment, my situation was truly not to be envied.

/Soon enough, the doors were opened to receive the first guests, followed shortly by the rest. I now had to do the honors as the hostess, however it might go. To be able to introduce the ladies to each other, I had spent several days beforehand practicing the correct pronunciations of their names. The unfamiliar sounds made the task quite difficult, and I constantly mixed up the names in the beginning. When the soup was announced, the gentlemen came and offered their arms to each of the ladies, even though they were, of course, complete strangers. The usual practice for such events was to alternate the seating of ladies and gentlemen at the table. With such a divergent, yes, even diametrically opposed way of life, relative to what I was used to, I felt—quite naturally, of course—your disapproval every time. And you can believe me that it put my soul in turmoil every time.

/But what could someone in my position do differently? And so, I just had to "howl with the wolves." For if I had wanted to act otherwise, who knows how that would have been received, and I was sure to become a very uncomfortable half of the marriage for my husband. In front of every lady's plate stood a small bouquet in a glass, which I had placed there myself an hour before. Who can describe my feelings when the servant asked me: "Madam, bouillon or mock turtle soup?"—That was too cruel! How could I have had the heart to enjoy the meat of my silent companion? Of course, I chose the bouillon.

If there is something I find especially disagreeable about these social gatherings, then I will name two things: First, how much and how loud people talk while eating, often making it hard to hear what your neighbor is saying, and then—how much they drink. You cannot even imagine the totality of what people drink here. Often enough, the matter has left me simply disgusted. How amazing people are with their countless customs; in the Tropics, they first consume their meals completely and then drink some water afterwards. In the North, by contrast, it seems to me that people drink more than they eat. It struck me as very unnatural to have to drink so much wine, without really being thirsty. No wonder that people get all too loud and seek to override each other in conversation. Here this condition is called an "animated gathering," although I very much doubt you can fully grasp this description.

People very much liked my curry, at least those who had been in the Orient and were familiar with the dish. Happily, I was able to converse a considerable amount on this day in Hindustani as well as Swahili, since some of our guests understood those languages.

Now it was time for the unavoidable toasts. You would surely like to know what this word means, would you not? I was no wiser than you initially about the importance of this practice, that at virtually every meal a gentleman suddenly taps on his glass before standing up and embarking on a long speech, while all the guests listen with rapt attention. On such occasions, the speaker loftily intones the virtues of the hosts, whether justified or not, something listeners are, as a rule, left to decide for themselves. The end of the speech typically results in a scene that a foreigner, such as me, is hard-pressed to describe. Chairs are pushed back, and the whole group appears to rise up, as if on command, to clink each other's wine glasses. This ritual is usually conducted rather noisily, so much so that I hardly knew what to make of the scene the first time I experienced it. Having been so richly praised and flattered, the host must then naturally respond in kind, as described above, to express his thanks. My head would start spinning so much on these occasions that I was always happy when people left the table and went into another room.

After our guests left, and my husband informed me that they had apparently spoken very appreciatively of our gathering, I was somewhat relieved that we had not embarrassed ourselves all too much, despite my private fears for days on end. And so I was truly happy to have successfully survived my opening debut in my own house in this quite highbrow Hamburg. I had to tell myself that if there are but a few people in the world who might refrain from criticizing others, then even they would be least likely to overlook the mistakes of someone they considered a totally uncultivated Arab woman.

You have no idea how difficult and complex European life was for me in the beginning, the thousand cliffs that confronted me everywhere, under conditions that were primed to cause my untrained feet to stumble. That Europeans come to us, to a setting where they are always able to maintain their lifestyles, struck me as child's play in comparison to my situation. Here, they constantly put obstacles in my way, which I had to tacitly work around, so as not to appear too helpless in the eyes of others. In a state of mind that still felt like I was barely awake, I was bombarded with never-ending impressions that hit me so quickly, one after another, that I felt like I was caught in a dream. There were just too many things that needed to be grasped and managed as quickly as possible if I hoped to make my life halfway tolerable in this completely strange setting. The prevailing conditions gave me no indulgence and no mercy; I had no choice but to cope and make do. Everything initially seemed so impossibly difficult, especially considering that so much went against my grain, and yet I still had to conform.

/Oh, how often did I wish we could have stayed in lovely Marseille, where I had felt so secure in the company of Madame M. and her niece. Nothing is harder to bear than to have to fight with oneself. And yet, it is good not to reveal all the apprehensions and doubts of our beleaguered souls every day, for this cold world seldom has a proper appreciation for what we feel and perceive most deeply. Only our true friends care about our personal joys and cares, not the alien world. At that point in time, all my friends, my husband being the sole exception, were basically antipodally distant from me.

/Had I, for example, been born and raised in Constantinople or Cairo, where European culture made inroads long ago, I may not have found such a stark contrast between Occident and Orient. In both cities, it was already long-established good form to engage European governesses to raise growing daughters, who were cultivated with various European languages, as well as music. Food there is also served forthrightly *à la franca*, meaning at a table with knives and forks. And as far as outfits and upkeep in the palaces, there is hardly any difference left to be found between Mohammedan and Parisian ladies. Should fate ever destine another Mohammedan from Constantinople or Cairo to be transplanted to Europe under the same circumstances as me, she would not even remotely be subjected to the same upheaval I have had to undergo. Had I not, until then, still been wearing the clothes of my great-ancestors from a thousand years ago and used my five fingers as natural knives and forks.

/The very slow progress of my German left me impatient. Things would get much easier, I had to tell myself, once I gained some ability to communicate with others. Most of all, I envied the people who went to Sunday church with their hymnals in the summer, while we took off on another outing. I had this deep desire to finally get to know how Christians pray to their God, and so I asked my husband to go to church with me. One Sunday we then went, but as I stood at the door, ready to go in, I had the feeling I was about to do something wrong. I had no choice now but to enter, though, if I did not want to disgrace myself toward my husband.

/Having taken my place on a pew between other congregants, I was overcome with an indescribable feeling of trepidation, which continued to worsen as I realized that the church service kept on going. I naturally could not understand a word of what was being sung and said. But the sense that I was with the All-Holy soon calmed me. More than anything, though, I disliked the images in the church, first because it is strictly prohibited for us to pray in a room with any kind of picture, and second because I found they distracted me from my devotion, which I considered sinful. The fact that the worshippers showed no outward sign of humility toward the Almighty, by which I mean they did not prostrate themselves, struck me as very strange and arrogant; I found it very off-putting. Moreover, when I saw that money was being collected in the middle of prayer, my sensibilities, albeit completely uncultured from a Western perspective, registered nothing but desecration. I must openly admit that I consider it truly profane to call for money in a church and during a church service. One would think that, as soon as someone enters the house of the Lord, naught but a single thought would prevail, that every soul would give itself over totally and devoutly to God, and not that this place, of all places, would become a reminder of this worldly Mammon. Praying in the midst of several hundred people was also completely new for me.

/9

The first winter in the North did me no favors. I came down with a cough that refused to leave me for half a year. As a result, I learned the value of handkerchiefs, which everyone in these parts carries—like our talismans—everywhere they go. The time for Christmas was gradually getting closer, and these often foggy, sun-starved days put me in an indescribably despondent mood. To this day, even after so many years, the weather still has a great effect on my well-being. Whenever there was one of those rare sunny days in the winter, I would feel so much better. Later I also completely understood why the English suffer—as is said of them—from the "spleen" precisely in November and December. A dreary, foggy day could make me so melancholy that I often just wanted to cry.[47]

/The way people rushed about on the streets with their countless packages, the closer Christmas came, made such an impression on me that I pestered my husband with questions. For one, it was completely new to me that people would ask each other what gifts they wanted. As an example: "Friedrich, my son, what would you like for Christmas?" or also "Dear Anna, is there anything I can give you as a present?" and more of the same. I was therefore quite surprised when my husband asked me one day what I might in fact desire and what I most wanted to have. Of course, I had absolutely no specific wishes, since I had everything I might need. We now often went into town to make purchases for my husband's relatives and our servants. In general, I really enjoyed the way everyone, from the highest to the lowest, could make their own purchases. This struck me as much better and more comfortable than our way of doing it, which makes us so dependent on the taste and intelligence of our slaves.

/Until now, I was used to buying things only together with my husband, so I found it very difficult to get something for him for Christmas without his knowledge. How could it have been otherwise, since I still did not understand German, much less speak it. I wanted to give him a golden pocket watch, since his no longer worked very well. One day I gathered enough courage to go into town alone at a time when I knew he would be busy in his office and could not easily run into me on the street. After I had studied the lovely shops on

---

47 In historical understandings of the human body, melancholia (from the Greek for "black" and "bile") was one of the four temperaments that matched the four humors, each tied to a human organ. If the spleen produced too much black bile, that was said to create an imbalance with blood, phlegm, and yellow bile that would lead to a melancholic temperament. Under humorism, black bile corresponded to the cold and dry conditions of autumn.

the Jungfernstieg and Neuer Wall[48] from the outside for a while, not without a heavily beating heart, I slipped into a watch store and found myself standing somewhat helplessly in front of the storekeeper. He bowed politely and began to speak to me, which of course was beyond my comprehension. My only response was to point to the pretty watches he kept in his case. This poor watchmaker looked at me quizzically, apparently not quite knowing what to do with me. He shook his head and proceeded to simply seat himself again. This impolite treatment did not suit me at all and so I persisted with my pointing. Finally, he conceded and opened the case for me. I then began to canvass my options, all the while feeling how this man kept a sharp eye on me. Who knows if he did not at that moment consider me a store thief.

/Having now found a watch that I liked, we encountered major problems with the payment. It proved impossible to reach an understanding, at which point I lost my patience and grabbed this startled man by the arm, rubbed my thumb and pointer finger together, our way of signifying payment, and simultaneously pointed to the door. Nearby I knew a very famous jeweler, who I hoped could help me out of this dilemma. I spoke the jeweler's name to the watchmaker, and lo and behold, his face lit up, despite having previously looked at me so skeptically. And thus we actually walked out the door, the watchmaker bearing my chosen watch, to the jeweler in question with whom I had good credit, to ask him to enable the transaction with the watchmaker. Later, this jeweler could not get enough of telling my husband the tale of this very funny situation we had found ourselves in. Quietly triumphant, I headed back home, although not before buying a couple of *berloques*[49] for the watch from the jeweler, my rescuer in time of need. The whole way home I was beset with concern that I might still happen to run into my husband on the street and spill my secret in an untimely fashion. It would have been too easy for him to figure me out, since I never liked to go out without him.

/On Christmas Eve, after our servants had gotten their presents, we drove off in a carriage to my husband's parents with their presents, to spend the evening there. It was my first Christmas celebration ever, and to this point, I had absolutely no idea how Christians celebrate their festivals. I was acutely interested in finding out what this Occidental ritual was like. I had seen pictures in the church, but without knowing their meaning and purpose, and not having

---

48 The author refers to two perpendicular streets in Hamburg: first, the beautiful waterfront avenue that lines the Binnenalster and second, a major avenue that remains one of Europe's top luxury shopping streets. Reconstructed after the great fire of 1842, the Jungfernstieg and adjoining area acquired a horse tram line in 1867, just as the Ruete newlyweds moved in on the other side of the Außenalster.
49 From the French, meaning small trinket or charm, usually worn on a chain or bracelet.

wanted to ask my husband about them—on the one hand, out of consideration for his feelings toward his religion (for what did I know back then of the countless ways to profess one's Christianity?), and on the other hand—and that was the main thing for me—to avoid discovering that the Christian religion was in fact, as some tended to believe in our parts, idol worship. Exactly that would have been contrary to my convictions. For these reasons, I steered clear of any questions pertaining to the upcoming celebration.

/On our drive, we passed one of the busiest streets in the city, with people whose rushed pace could hardly be described as walking. The whole world seemed to be in such an inexplicable hurry. I will never forget the scene of a man, tightly gripping a pendulum clock with both arms, who rushed along with such speed that everyone scurried out of his way. When the carriage stopped, I could see an array of heads looking down at us from the second floor. My husband's younger brothers came out and helped us carry the presents into the house. Once we had reached the upstairs, I found everything so secretive, and there was no end to the whispering. I was strictly forbidden to enter the dining room, which heightened my curiosity even more. And then we heard a bell ringing out from that mysterious room, whereupon the younger generation jubilantly ran in. "Bibi!" my husband called, "Emily!" the others called, and so we all went in.

/There I stood, in front of a tree filled with so many burning lights and draped with all sorts of sweets. Now I was led to a table on which all sorts of things had been stacked for me. But I completely missed the main present, until my dear husband said to me: "Bibi, this is also for you." Only then did I take a closer look. It was a large velvet coat, lined with fur and trimmed from top to bottom, including the sleeves, with ermine. You can imagine my amazement when I saw what was from a European point of view the most precious of coats. Really—I thought to myself—of all things, I am to wear fur here, which only the wildest of our native Africans would ever wear? No, for my husband to expect that of me would be too extreme. I could not help but say to him in Swahili: "Is it possible that I am actually supposed to wear this thing, and that you, of all people, would give it to me?" "Please, Bibi," came the answer, "this is something especially fine. The outer fur is called ermine and is usually worn only by royals." "Royals, you say, wear this? But why? Are the princes and princesses here so poor, as poor as our native Africans in Zanzibar?" "Oh no, surely not," he responded with laughter. "Indeed, ermine is the height of luxury here." I must confess that it took me a long time before I could accustom myself to this cloak of European royalty. Back then, the only value this ermine fur had for me was exactly the same as—the fur of a cat.

Shall I now tell you what I thought of this first Christmas celebration? Well, it is a tricky matter to comment on the customs and traditions of other peoples without now and again offending the latter, even if unintended. I only want to tell you my personal impressions, as I perceived them, but nothing more. For although I had previously considered the Protestant religion to be one of the most easygoing, and personally would have preferred somewhat greater formality, I found to my disappointment that the whole point of the Christmas Eve celebration was entirely overlooked. It astonished me to hear that the birth of Christ was being celebrated without even a single thought of prayer. Can you even imagine that? Surely not easy, and yet it is so. I was, as I said, very disappointed and would gladly have had fewer presents in exchange for a short religious ceremony. Of course, at the time I would have understood next to nothing, but even just the sight of a devotional would have sufficed for me to turn to prayer in my own way. From that time on, it became quite clear to me that being Christian was a relative term. Accordingly, my inner struggle grew more and more excruciating every day. I thought of our festivals, and my thoughts shot like arrows over to you—as if I could seek what I was missing amongst you!

/The next morning, on the 25th of December, my husband was surprised to see me coming down the stairs from the bedroom already at ten o' clock in my full regalia. He shouted something to me like: "My God, Bibi, what has happened, where on earth do you plan to go?" I first swooshed calmly down the stairs with my long train and then asked if he had not himself said to me that today and tomorrow were holidays. "As you see, that is why I got so dressed up." "Yes, Bibi, that is customary for you, but not here with us." Strange people, these Northerners, I thought to myself, and went back upstairs to change into my normal clothing. The way we prepare very special meals and cakes for festivals, they do the same.

So as not to offend my husband, I followed his wishes and had to wear this monstrous fur coat on our next outing. How that made me feel you can tell yourself without difficulty. And if a thief had conveniently thought to come to our house to steal this coat, I would surely have let him conduct his business without interfering in any way.

On New Year's Eve, I had a pretty shock when confronted with a totally drunk servant girl. According to the usual German custom, my husband had prepared the indispensable New Year's punch for himself and his brothers, of which our servants each received a glassful. For my part, the first sip did nothing for me, as with all strong drinks, so I completely refrained. When I wanted to head to bed as usual at ten o' clock, I rang for the servant girl, for her to light the upstairs. She let me wait an unusually long time, so I went into the corridor to call her up from the basement. At long last, she dragged her way up the stairs and slurred several times: "Madam, Madam!" Only a few more stairs to reach me—and this punch-indulging character collapsed into a heap. Since I had thus far fortunately never had such direct exposure to a drunkard and only heard talk of such godless people, which is what we call them, I let out a noteworthy scream, causing my husband to rush out of the dining room to me. From then on, I took note of how much punch every servant girl could bear on New Year's Eve, having learned from this experience. What do you think about such a thirst and even more, such a throat?

Early on, I found the sight of thousands of people ice skating on the frozen river truly magical. I could not get enough of watching the people, who seemed equipped with some sort of invisible wings, from our front yard. An extraordinarily talented young girl among our acquaintances seemed to me just like a sailing ship tacking against wind and weather. Great efforts were also made to teach me how to skate, but sadly to no avail, since my clumsy feet, which move very awkwardly on icy surfaces even to this day, could not master the challenge. Much later, I had a gentleman tell me when he noticed my inability in this art: "Ah, Madam, you are not so easily led onto the ice?"[50] How witty this man must have thought himself in making this joke!

Summer finally arrived. Although the warmth was not quite exhilarating, it was a much better fit for the never-ending hustle and bustle on the part of all of humanity here in this land, as compared to an excessively hot season. I was filled with childish joy by the first leaves on the trees, which had looked like broomsticks for almost six months, giving newcomers the impression that they had all suddenly dried out and were waiting to be cut down. I was so happy to be able to sit in the yard again, or generally outdoors, for after months of sitting in heated rooms, and only occasionally letting in the fresh air, I had really had more than enough. In these rooms, I frequently felt so pinned in and pent up that I often stretched my whole head out of the window, even in the biting cold, just to breathe in some air. But I could tolerate this sport only a few minutes at a time, since the indescribably cold air quickly propelled me back in again. Often enough, this craving for fresh air left me feeling quite sick.

This was also the time when everyone asked each other, "And what are your summer plans?" We, or more specifically my husband, also faced these questions. When he translated for me, I was quite surprised to hear that

---

50 The German expression cited by the author—*aufs Eis führen*—is idiomatic for duping someone.

everyone—of course, only if they had the necessary funds—made it a point to leave the city for several months. When I asked him if we also had to travel, I was very happy to hear the comforting answer from my kindhearted and always accommodating husband that, if I preferred not to go anywhere, he would be happy to stay at home. Surely you also want to know why people leave the city in the summer and where they go. In the big European cities, there are houses and apartments that have absolutely no trees or bushes in their vicinity. Indeed, there are even living spaces, the so-called inner court and cellar apartments, where the residents—pity them!—barely see any sky. And precisely those people are so impoverished and in such need that fate condemns them to live and die there.

/ So the well-to-do class goes to the countryside or to the coast to indulge in some of summer and, as people also like to say here, recover from the winter. Later I also had the chance to participate in these so-called recuperation trips. Traveling when schools are on vacation is the worst, worse than you can possibly imagine. Both coming and going, it is a relief not to simply be crushed in the railway compartments, and it is best not to elaborate on the frequently prevailing atmosphere. During these travel periods, there is such a hustle and bustle at the train stations that it often feels like Judgment Day is coming, as taught to us in the Koran.

After eleven months of instruction for two hours every day, I finally began to understand some German, enough that I soon thereafter ended my lessons. Grammar, however, seemed to pose such insurmountable obstacles for me that I was happy to leave it to my devoted teacher. The German language is tougher than most, and its grammar is a hard nut for the novice to crack, one that takes so much time to overcome. Given my ignorance of the usual arrangements, language, and more, it was to be expected that our good servants would do their utmost to enrich themselves at our expense. We were in essence completely in their hands for almost two years and lived in our own house during that time much like in a hotel. We seldom knew exactly what we would be served. Not until seated at the table did we get to see what they deemed adequate for us to eat.

/As bad behavior seldom prospers, it eventually became clear how much these people had taken advantage of us. Once I became aware, I considered it my duty to look after things, as much as I could. The first thing I did was send all the old servants away. They had demonstrated their disloyalty more than enough and naturally could not be retained, not a one, so as not to set a bad example for the new domestics. From then on, I kept the household book, in German of course, but please do not ask me "how"! That it was filled with countless errors, and the script was of dubious legibility, you can well imagine. I took charge of the household funds, handled all expenditures, ordered the necessary provisions, and made up the daily grocery list myself. As I undertook my new task, my abilities gradually grew. Less than half a year after taking up this new position, I received my husband's praise, for by then we were eating no worse than before, but living at about half the cost of what it took when our servants still ruled.

In the third summer of our time in Hamburg, my husband proposed that we take a trip to Copenhagen. The plan was to travel without our two children, which did not suit me at all. The idea of leaving one's small children behind, for no reason, with the youngest being only four months old,[51] was completely incomprehensible to me. And yet, it was to be a pleasure trip. It is, I suppose, rather naïve of me to admit that I actually spent the night before this "pleasure trip" sleepless and in tears. We were meant to be away from the children for only two weeks, and yet, that seemed far too long for me. The thought of leaving the children behind, just for me to have a little fun, struck me as so heartless. When I asked, what on earth was the point of going to Copenhagen, I received an answer that I did not well understand. I could not be with the children forever, so I might as well start getting used to that. Does that make any sense to you? Certainly not to me. Not even when my dear husband told me about a Mrs. C., who had only recently left with her husband for China, and for several years at that, while calmly leaving her children back in Hamburg.

/I could see that resistance was futile, especially as my husband appeared to take such stock in having me come along. On this occasion, he jokingly claimed that I loved the children more than him, which was of course not true. And so, we arrived happily in Copenhagen, and the first thing we visited was the Museum of Thorwaldsen. I saw so many beautiful things here for the first time, but they left no impression on me. Even the concert in Clamlenburg, where the royal family was in attendance, had no effect on me, as my thoughts were constantly with my children. And in the end, rather than stay the entire two weeks as planned, we hurried home after just a week. I believe no living soul was happier than I was that day when I could once again press my young children to my heart.

My first reading material in the German language was newspaper advertisements. I was quite proud of this accomplishment, especially as I had initially been quite sure that learning this language would be impossible for me.

---

51 Her youngest at the time was her son Said, later called Rudolph. Rosa, her youngest daughter and last child, was born the next year.

Time passed without any noteworthy events for me. Only once did I experience a small shock, which fortunately passed quite quickly. Namely, we came close to moving to Valparaiso. My ability to stay in touch with you all would have been significantly challenged from America. Plus for now, I had had more than enough with my transition to Germany, even if the Chilean climate would have suited me much better. So we stayed in Germany.

/In the spring of 1870, it turned out that my husband needed to travel to England for a couple of weeks on business. Our youngest child at the time was barely six weeks old, so I naturally needed to stay at home. But that was easier said than done, for the mere thought of having to rely entirely on myself in this foreign setting, even for just a short while, put me into such a state of anxiety that I begged my husband to take me and the children along. "No, Bibi, that really is not possible," was his answer, "because I need to visit many towns in England, and you cannot join me everywhere. But you will see that I will be back in two weeks, at most three!" My husband did what he could to assuage my inexplicable, even to me, fear of staying in Hamburg alone without him.

I expect you may be asking yourself why it took so long for me to get used to my new environment. Please do not judge me too rashly, and believe me, adapting to a people that is so very different is more easily contemplated than practiced. On the outside, I gave as little cause as possible for anyone to think I was challenged, but on the inside, I never stopped feeling lonely and vulnerable when my husband was gone. A sign of how much you all still occupied my thoughts during this time—when I was still unencumbered and fortunate that my husband treated me with such love and devotion—is evident from the fact that I dreamt exclusively of you all, night after night. Oh, how often did my husband tease me when I was ready to turn in somewhat earlier, for he would say: "Aha, Bibi, do you want to travel to Zanzibar so soon today? Then please give my best to our friends there." The three weeks passed by very slowly, and I was happy when my husband returned back home.

10

A few weeks later, the great war between Germany and France broke out,[52] which caused tremendous excitement for everyone. We were assigned soldiers to be quartered in our home for a short time, but opted to avoid the related inconvenience by lodging them in a simple inn. Now began a war between the two nations that you, on your peaceful island, cannot fathom. Hundreds upon hundreds of thousands of people were sacrificed on both sides. Somewhat in the manner that the devout Muslims, during their annual pilgrimage, sacrifice countless sheep on Mount Arafat, where it is said our father Adam and our mother Eve met again after being expelled from Paradise.[53] When the war erupted, people here were as if electrified, for all the talk was of the war and nothing else. One has to marvel at the patriotism of the Germans, since their sacrifice of blood and goods was virtually unlimited at the time. What offerings of men and money such a war consumes mocks any description. To undertake such a war of attrition—nota bene: Christians against Christians—Europeans start to train their male youth already at a very early age for this purpose.

/All European states suffer more or less from the same very bad malady, namely jealousy. No one grants the others anything, and every state always strives to be ahead of every other state, no matter the cost. Every state, even the very smallest, has its own host of spies, who are tasked with reconnoitering their dear neighbors. And naturally, all the statesmen are constantly striving to assure each other that they are not aware of the existence of any such individuals. Efforts are made across the board to invent the most terrible instruments of mass murder, in order to take the first opportunity to duly impress one's own power upon the neighbor, without diminishing the lovely-sounding words by which the statesmen mutually assure each other of the sincerity of their goodwill.

/Woe to any nation that has the misfortune today of losing a war. On top of all its material losses, the ruthless imposition of taxes poses an added threat, as a screw that gets turned ever tighter, depending on how great the need or desire. Under these circumstances, it has always seemed to me that the so-called humanitarian principles in Europe were mainly studied and applied to free the

---

52 The author is referring to the Franco-Prussian War from July 1870, when France declared war, to January 1871, when France surrendered, followed by the Treaty of Frankfurt in May 1871.
53 Mount Arafat is also known as the Mount of Mercy because, as some Muslims believe, the Lord forgave Adam and Eve when they reunited and repented there. He then also promised to forgive any of their offspring who subsequently appeared there on the same day, the day before the Big Festival or Great Bayram. *Memoirs*, p. 148.

slaves. But what does it mean for one African state to fight and raid another when compared to a single war in the North! The view here is that when a nation loses a war, its wings must also be clipped, to create a crippling effect that will endure a minimum of many years hence. And what an outcry there is here about the slaves we keep, even though these slaves are far better off than some of the people here. As you know, we are not remotely social democrats, and yet I have often had to consider whether it would be more appropriate if the individual European governments were to spend their countless millions on their own impoverished populations, who suffer such privation, especially in the winter, instead of using the money for the so-called "liberation" of Africans. But all this is mostly decided at the usual green table,[54] which is to say by people who know just about as much about Africans, their temperaments, and their needs as you and I know about the inhabitants of other planets.

/Nowhere does the contrast between the haves and have nots appear greater than right here in the cold North, where one finds, on the one hand, such opulence and luxury, and on the other, such heart-rending poverty. I once saw such poverty in the case of an unemployed coach driver's family, who had absolutely nothing but a number of freezing and hungry children! When I saw this misery, for which I unfortunately had no means of providing a durable remedy, and could only provide momentary relief, I was so seized by this plight the entire day that I could hardly eat. I could not help but think that out of a hundred of our slaves, not even two would want to exchange their lot with this kind of freedom.

/And what indeed is the military draft if not a type of slavery, a system that, with the exception of England, is highly nurtured across all of Europe. As a result, when war breaks out in a country where this system of obligatory military service prevails, the male population from 17 to 45 years of age is, as needed, pulled into the field. This arrangement also signifies great justice, with no distinction made between rich and poor, or the son of a prince and the son of a cobbler. Even Jews must go to war, just like Christians. With this constant preparation and the ongoing new procurements for the military, the State takes on expenditures that completely exceed your ability to comprehend. For entirely impartial outsiders, meaning people who have no association with Christianity and know of the peaceful, love-thy-neighbor teachings of Jesus only through books and stories, it must appear totally incongruous to watch

---

54 The German expression used by the author—*etwas am gruenen Tisch entscheiden*—refers to people sitting at the classic leather- or cloth-covered green table (picture today's billiard tables) and making out-of-touch decisions in the official, bureaucratic meeting room.

how its adherents seek to outdo each other in who can invent the deadliest and most *en gros* annihilating weapon. But this is called progress here. You, however, in your simplicity, if you were to consider all these arts that they call progress here, were you to see all of it and everything that goes with it, I am entirely sure you would call them—simply satanic.

Stereograph entitled "Red fields of slaughter sloping down to ruin's black abyss"

11

In this tumultuous time of war between Germany and France, I was struck, as you know, by the greatest tragedy of my life. During this period, I was just beginning to gradually get used to the climate, the people, the food, and the until-then completely unfamiliar conditions, when fate delivered me such a powerful blow. The way we usually feel safe from any storm under a clear and cloudless sky, that is how I felt shortly before my misfortune. I happened to be lying in bed with a fever, where I needed to be given cold compresses for my head to combat the heat resulting from weaning my youngest child. Beyond that, there was no sign of what was to come.

On this day, I felt somewhat better, and so my husband opted to set out on a visit to his sick father, who was staying in his summer cottage and could be reached only by horse-drawn rail. He returned from the office as usual at four o' clock and then left me to go downstairs at half past four to eat his lunch alone. Shortly thereafter, he left the house, and I fell into a deep sleep. When I awoke, it was already completely dark. The nanny brought the children to my bed to say good night. Until nine o' clock, I lay there peacefully, without any concern, knowing to expect my husband's return during that time. But from then on, I was gripped by a totally inexplicable fear, which also grew from minute to minute. I was too spoiled by his exemplary punctuality, in addition to the fact that he almost never went out for supper, unlike so many others. I listened with strained breathing to the regular call of the steamboats in the Alster, which passed right by our front yard, and each time, I imagined that he might have gone into town with the horse tram and then continued by steamboat out to us.

/But all remained still, and no one pulled at the doorbell, so as to calm my heart perhaps for just an instant, while it pounded with such foreboding. Around eleven, I succumbed to a cold fever and lay there shivering, barely able to exchange even a sound with the nanny. Midnight struck, and my husband still had not returned. A thousand thoughts coursed through my head in my already agitated feverish state, and one scary scene chased another. I suspected some calamity by now all too clearly, and my fever-exacerbated fantasy drew up the most horrid images, for I knew my husband only too well, that he would never intentionally cause me to be afraid, especially now when I was sick. Every instant, I wanted to get up and at least walk up and down our street in case I might run into him. But each time, I forced myself, with effort, to give up the thought. This night remains forever unforgettable, as it counts for years of my life.

Then finally—the quiet sound of the doorbell being pulled. Thanks be to the Lord! evoked my soul, for here he has now finally come. Naturally he pulled softly on the bell, so as not to wake me from my sleep, I thought to myself, and waited with tense nerves for his familiar footsteps. Five minutes passed, seemingly an eternity, and yet I heard nothing. This, too, struck me as so strange, so peculiar, since it was his usual custom, as soon as he got home and deposited his hat and coat in the wardrobe, to immediately seek me out in one room after another until he found me. At this time, he would have come straight up to the bedroom, so late at night—or so I calculated.

/When, however, everything continued in silence, I felt such an indescribable fear and dread arise anew that I suddenly sprang out of my bed, just as I was. Without pulling anything more on, only in my long English nightgown, I ran down the corridor and loudly began calling my husband. I took the opportunity to bend deeply over the banister for him to hear me more clearly, when I suddenly felt myself being grabbed tightly by the servant girl, who had come leaping up the stairs. "Where is the master, where is my husband, Anna, where is my husband?" I called to the girl, who was very flush in the face. I wanted to free myself from her and rush down the stairs, for now it appeared all too clear that something had happened to him. This foreboding at first seemed to practically rob me of my sanity, and so I exerted extra-human effort to try to pull myself away to reach the stairs, as the nanny and cook, who had also rushed over, sought to remove me from the banister. Meanwhile one of them tried to comfort me with words that gave me little relief: "Madam, calm yourself, the master is still alive, but he is very sick!" That was too much for my fever-impacted body, and I apparently collapsed. My otherwise robust nerves gave out for just a short while, though, and when I opened my eyes again, still dazed, I saw a male stranger standing before me.

/"Madam," began the gentleman with emotion rising in his voice, "take courage, your husband still lives, for he is the one who sent me here." "Where is my husband? I want to see him!" I repeatedly pressed my question, as yet unaware how great my misfortune was. "Madam, do you recognize me? I am of course R., your neighbor's house doctor." And yet he still hesitated to answer my question, even as I posed it again and again. His hesitation signified only disaster, and so I implored him, as much as I could in German, to tell me everything quickly and truthfully. Whereupon he shared enough detail that I could see how very dire the disaster was.

/For this is what happened: My husband was on the way home, returning from his sick father, on the horse tram. When he got to the end of the line, which was still a ways from our home, he jumped, as is unfortunately the habit of all gentlemen here, from the open platform in the front and fell with such disadvantage that he was gripped by the still-moving tram and—overrun! And even though he was fatally injured, he did not lose his powerful strength right away, as he went on his own by foot to a nearby carriage stop, had the carriage call on Doctor R., who happened to live in the area, and then rode with the same to the next hospital. Upon arrival, he was given emergency care. He then bade Doctor R. to ride to me, so as to let me know of the events in the gentlest way possible. And thus it was midnight before I learned of the accident. How badly my husband was injured and how dangerous his injuries were, of that the Doctor naturally said nothing. But from his tone and compassionate manner with which he tried to comfort me, I could feel and guess the magnitude of the damage enough.

/Against all reason and overcome by an indescribable fear, I demanded on the spot, in the very form I had left my bed, to go to my husband. "No, Madam, that is not possible. They would never even let you into the hospital so late at night!" That was the Doctor's answer. I responded, however, that if he was not willing to take me in his carriage to my husband, I would go the whole long

One of the first horse-drawn trams in Hamburg, late 1860s.

distance on foot. And if then the people at the hospital were so hardhearted as to keep me from seeing my husband, I would rather spend the night under the open sky at the hospital door than stay here in this house. When the sympathetic Doctor now realized that I would not be held back, he finally said: "Well, Madam, at the very least you must get yourself properly dressed, or you may otherwise end up freezing to death." After having hurriedly added the minimal clothing, I ran more than walked down the stairs and drove with the Doctor and the nanny to the hospital.

/Oh, my God, what a ride! Everything seemed to progress so slowly, the horse, the carriage, even the driver seemed half asleep to me. My mind had already reached the hospital long before, and my sick fantasy mercilessly painted the absolute worst images before my eyes. I cannot conjure up the right words to adequately describe my state of being, since there are pains that can only be experienced, where words do not suffice. May the good Lord preserve everyone from such a trip.

/Finally, after barely half an hour, the carriage reached its destination. Dear Doctor R. led me in and then looked for the supervisor. The latter arrived, but seemed very ill-disposed that I had come. When I noticed that, I went down on my knee and begged: "Oh, Mr. Supervisor, please take compassion and let me go to my poor husband." "That is not allowed," he answered, "and patients can be visited only on certain days during certain hours." "What?" I said, "I may not see my husband any time soon?" Oh my God, how hard and unfeeling people are here. What an imposition, that total strangers would suddenly take the power upon themselves to stand between me and my husband, callously uncaring about my unspeakable despair.

/Permission and policy! How I could have cared less for those two words in that instant, for I found myself in such desperation that law, authority, and the whole world seemed entirely non-existent. I was not far from losing my sanity altogether that night. Later my female companion told me how I had run along the endless hospital corridors, back and forth, from one end to the other, exclaiming my misery in a foreign language, of which I subsequently had no memory. I was now no longer willing to let myself be sent off without first having seen my husband again, even if only briefly. For who could know, other than the Almighty himself, if I would ever, subject to all these complete strangers and their countless rules, see him alive again. They would have had to carry me out the door to make me leave the hospital, since I certainly would not have gone on my own.

/One needs to have been born and raised in Europe to be able to subordinate oneself to the thousand limitations that so frequently infringe on personal liberties and simply turn the individual person into a number. Such compulsion does not fit us primitive peoples, since we mostly put our hearts first and then apply cold calculations.

Finally, the supervisor showed some mercy and promised his willingness to take me to my husband on the condition that I stay at most a quarter hour and generally keep my composure. Were I to follow his terms, I could come again to visit my husband tomorrow. Even so, I had to wait a very long time until the hospital surgeon, Doctor C., arrived to properly diagnose and bind the countless deadly wounds. The humane supervisor tried to comfort me in the meantime, which was apparently not easy for him, since he had a kind, soft heart, and I often saw how surreptitiously tried to dry his moist eyes.

/When Doctor C. had finally finished with the poor patient, what seemed an eternity to me, the supervisor returned and led me to the sick room. It was kept largely in darkness, and as I entered with trembling limbs, I almost lost my breath. In this moment, I could not have emitted a single sound, even if it had cost my whole being. With difficulty, I approached his bed, from which I heard an eternally unforgettable voice: "*Bibi, roho jangu!*" (Bibi, my soul, my life, my breath), before I could catch myself. "You still came so late, be brave, my life, and do not cry so!" I could muster but a few words in response: "Are you in great pain?" "Yes, very much!" "Where?" "On my chest." "What happened?" "*Amury ja mungu!*" (By God's will.) I barely dared speak any more, much less ask more questions, for I saw how difficult it was for him. So I sat in the half-darkened room and had to very much strain my eyes to make out the beloved features. One of his hands held mine tightly, without my suspecting that the other arm, which lay under the blanket, was completely shattered. I would learn more the next day.

/It took about half an hour before the supervisor returned to pick me up, so that the patient could try to get some sleep. I cannot rightly express in words what feelings I had as I took my leave. We exchanged our "*jacu onana!*" (good-bye!), without much convincing energy from at least one of us, and I slunk more than walked out of the room on the arm of the supervisor. Outside in the corridor, the friendly supervisor let me know that I could stay with my husband from tomorrow onwards and that he would hold an adjoining room for me. Hearing these words with unspeakable gratitude, I simply threw my arms around the neck of this good old man.

I was so physically diminished that it took considerable effort for me to move. In the end, my strength completely left me, and I was half carried, half dragged by the nanny and the supervisor back to the carriage. The rest of the night I spent on the balcony in the open, since I could not tolerate my small room where I felt suffocated. Even though it was summer, the night was still so bitter cold. Wrapped in a thick throw, I sat there deep in my misery until the glittering stars, one after another, faded away to make room for the breaking dawn of the new day. Then I crept back into my room and waited for the children, one by one, to wake up. Upon seeing them, I became so unutterably sad that I broke down in uncomprehending tears, for a deep premonition told me only too clearly how soon they stood to lose the blessing of having a father.

/After assisting the nanny with bathing the children and their breakfast, I left for the hospital already at nine o' clock. Here I had to wait again for almost another hour in the supervisor's room, until the chief surgeon came to replace the patient's bandages. I approached the door of the sick room with a pounding heart and had to stand there for a long time before I found the courage to enter. Finally, I entered the room. There I found my husband still without fever and possessed with a clear understanding. But, oh how he looked! For now, in the bright light of a July day,[55] I could see immediately what had been obscured the night before. A large gash covered the length of his forehead, the nose was damaged, the back of his head revealed an even larger and more dangerous wound. One ear was completely gone. The fatal wound, however, lay on his chest, which along with his arm was thoroughly crushed. One leg was also very significantly damaged. I had to pull myself together to hide the shock and pain I was feeling. I would not have thought such deformity possible in such a short time! It seemed to me that he himself did not clearly understand the hopelessness of his situation, as he went on about all sorts of trivial things, which amazed me. And so I only too gladly allowed myself to be lightly deluded by his calm state and clear mind, and accordingly soon took heart again. Since it was late July, and the day was quite hot, I had brought along a handheld fan, which he himself had given to me in my homeland, to keep the flies off him. That brought us to recalling past days and events, with our thoughts drifting far off to the Equator.

---

55 This daytime visit appears to have been on July 30, 1870, based on the hospital intake report of the Allgemeine Krankenhaus St. Georg (General Hospital of St. Georg) from the prior day, discovered and kindly shared by Fridjof Gutendorf, as part of his extensive research in various Hamburg archives.

View of Zanzibar

I sat by his bedside, for the moment almost happy, until about two o' clock in the afternoon, when he suddenly became feverish and toward evening also began to fantasize. Under the circumstances, the doctors considered it better that I spend the night at home, as I also felt somewhat unwell, and then return the next morning. Although with a heavy heart, I followed their advice, if only to retain my hard-won advantages, as opposed to being able to see my patient only twice a week for short periods, as otherwise dictated by the harsh rules. I also longed to see the children again. When I arrived at home, all three were already in their beds and long asleep, which left me sitting at their bedsides where I could be persuaded of their healthy, regular breathing. The house seemed so barren and desolate. I felt like I was in someone else's home and could not sit still anywhere. In the end, I found my refuge in the children's room and stayed there.

The next morning, I returned to the hospital and arrived just as the church service was beginning (it happened to be a Sunday). I encountered many recovering patients on their way to the chapel. Oh, how full my heart was at that moment, all my feelings culminating in but a single thought, whether my husband would ever be granted the privilege of thanking the Lord in this same chapel for his own convalescence! Later, it was indeed a great comfort for me to have been together with him in church shortly before his accident. For even though I had barely understood the sermon, simply the thought of being in the Lord's house has always given me fulfillment and kept me from becoming discouraged.

/Today the kind supervisor greeted me with a glowing smile, as he told me that my husband had slept quite well and also asked for something to eat. And so it was; I found him not only without any fever, but also in good spirits. He had almost no pain, which struck me as very odd. He also hoped to be up and about again very soon. Encouraged by this positive turn of events, I asked the two assigned doctors to allow my husband to be transported to our house, since the transport itself could not do him much harm. I had noticed that a canal of the Alster flowed directly to the hospital, so that a boat ride right up to our front yard could be handled quite easily without much exertion by the patient. But the doctors categorically rejected my suggestion, saying "Absolutely not, your husband is not transportable." Nor did the doctors allow my suggestion that the patient's full beard, which was covered with blood and seemed to bother him greatly, should be shaved. "A few more days, Madam, and then it will happen." That was their answer. Toward evening, his condition again shifted so very rapidly that I could only leave him with growing concern, to return the next morning.

When I came back the next day, I found him very sick, as he had been feverish and delirious the entire night, and still was. On this day, I wore a white embroidered blouse, as was the fashion at the time. When my husband saw me coming, he indeed recognized me right away, but soon asked seriously, almost imploring, if I had gotten dressed so nicely to take him on a walk. And then he repeated these words several times: "*Ngodje kidogo, Bibi, mimi ntakuischa kuwa nguo sangu karidu!*" (Wait a moment, Bibi, I am almost done getting dressed!) His state deteriorated visibly, and three strong hospital staff had difficulty keeping him in bed, since he kept wanting to jump out.

/My heart bled indescribably as I watched him fight so wildly with these men, without my being able to help him. If it had been up to me, I surely would have left him alone, since the unnatural exertion was bound to cause him more harm than if he had been free to move around the room with sufficient oversight, as was the case here, until he would have ultimately tired himself out. I could see that the arm, which had been run over, and the leg as well, had turned a dark blue, but had no idea this was something bad. It was, in fact, a sign of gangrene, the name of this condition, something I had never previously heard of. No one made any effort to cure me of my ignorance, and I could hope as much as I pleased.

/For whom did I have that could have gradually prepared me for all that was to come? Absolutely no one. Small wonder then that I took no particular note of the increasingly blue appearance of the damaged limbs, with no inkling of the hopeless state the patient was in. This afternoon I begged the doctors to please grant me permission to spend the night with my patient, as it was impossible for me to find any peace, much less sleep, in my home and distant from him. But it was all for naught, since the smart doctors mostly show neither heart nor compassion.

With feelings I cannot describe, and deeply distressed, I again had to leave the hospital for the night. On the street, my carriage was stopped by an unfamiliar gentleman, even though the carriage was closed, and I sat deep in the back. The friendly old man inquired so empathetically about my husband, and as he closed the carriage door, I saw the bright tears flowing down his cheeks.

That night, my soul had all the feelings in the world for this hospital system and its leaders, except any good wishes! And since then, I have retained such an aversion to anything having to do with hospitals that it took me years to get over myself and enter one. Although in the evening, our house doctor, Doctor G., still stopped by, apparently to share some news, since I had not called for him, and he never simply came on his own. He was coming directly from my husband. This otherwise so worldly gentleman, who loved to tell jokes, was rather awkward today. He seemed to be avoiding my gaze and did not want to dwell on my questions about my husband. This all instilled in me an ever-increasing disquiet. When I pressed him to please tell me the absolute truth about my husband's condition and his own views of it, he visibly overcame his hesitation to say these few words: "Be strong, Madam, for there is no hope left!" Oh, that was enough for me. The doctor took his leave with sincere sympathy, and I was left alone with my misery.

/I must have sat there for hours without realizing that it was already late at night. When I finally came to my senses, my first impulse was to get down on my knees and plead fervently with the Almighty that if what the doctor had said was true, that there was now no hope left, that he accelerate my husband's demise, so as to free him from his anguish as quickly as possible. This time my wish was granted very soon.

/When I arrived at the hospital the next morning, the change was so great that the end was but a matter of hours. And although he momentarily recognized me, in that he spoke to me with these words: *"Heli gaeni, Bibi?"* (How are you, Bibi?), he soon reverted to an unconscious state. Around midday, his consciousness briefly returned, when he recognized me and asked for some fresh cherries. There were none to be had at this hour in the entire hospital, and by the time some were brought in from a store, it was sadly already much too late, since those had been his last conscious moments in this world. From that time on, I needed some years before I could again eat this fruit, which I had previously enjoyed so much. But in those early years, I gave the first cherries to the poor annually, exactly in the way, as you know, that we treat the favorite dishes of our dead. Oh, what I would have given in that hour for a handful of cherries! With pleasure, I would have offered up a few years of my life, and that certainly would not have been too much for me.

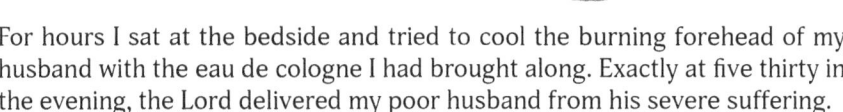

For hours I sat at the bedside and tried to cool the burning forehead of my husband with the eau de cologne I had brought along. Exactly at five thirty in the evening, the Lord delivered my poor husband from his severe suffering.

I would rather stay silent about this hour of my life because I have no words and not enough strength to recount what I suffered. At times, I abruptly lost my mental equilibrium, the only state in which I could have abandoned the almighty Creator. Bitterly, I accused him of allowing this untold misery to occur. I lost everything with my husband, yes everything—even the thought of my three children was not enough to comfort me. I suddenly stood there, forsaken and without a foundation, a wide chasm opening before my seeing eyes, seemingly pulling me in with all its might. Although I had prayed for an imminent release of my husband from his hardship, the hour came far too early for me. All preparations suddenly vanished, and the blow left me fully unprepared. Heaven and earth no longer existed for me then, and my soul was caught in an impenetrable desolation. Oh, what comfort I would have found at that moment in death! For what is a real death in relation to the boundless pain and suffering within ourselves! Nothing, absolutely nothing!

In the hospital, no one was interested in my desire to stay by the corpse until the burial. This struck me as beyond heartless. More dazed than awake, I drove back home where I experienced the bitter loss even more. Here at the stairs, I saw his sticks, his overcoat, his hats still hanging in the wardrobe, no one as yet having thought to remove them. I apparently also went through the whole house in a delirium, searching high and low, calling loudly for my husband. That he was dead, torn from me, never to be seen again, seemed more than I could comprehend or believe in my bottomless anguish. I was plagued by doubts that he was in fact gone. A secret voice kept saying to me: "Go on back to the hospital and get your husband; he is still alive!" "No, it cannot be true that he would have left you forever in this foreign land, hurry on over, hurry!" Oh, what insanity, what agony! I believed with complete certainty that all the doctors in the hospital had made a mistake and that my husband only appeared to be dead. And what now, if he were to come to his senses again and no one would be there with him? Would he not be aggrieved by my lack of loyalty, to have abandoned him precisely in such a moment? Oh, I could not bear it!

/I spent that night obsessively wandering the balcony and returned to the room only when I could no longer control myself, to hide my loud sobbing. Up in the firmament of the Eternal One, I furtively sought a sign, a miracle, to give my poor, struggling soul some small comfort. The nighttime calm and quiet, and the rustling leaves in the garden, even the stars shining in the sky, proved quite troubling to me that night. Nothing had changed outdoors, all of nature continued on as before; the only change was within me. I hoped for a calamity that would snatch me and my children away, to put an end to us as well. Just the thought of having to live alone with my small children in a foreign land, and without my husband, threatened to simply rob me of my sanity! Oh, and what that really meant! In all of Germany, yes, in all of Europe, I had not a single soul I could have leaned on for support, on top of my deficient German. The loss I had only recently suffered, of homeland, extended family, and possessions, and the youthful resilience with which I had borne it, only now revealed its true impact and reach. For at no point had my homesickness burned as severely as now. I could feel how, in an instant, I went to having no homeland and no relatives. Inconsolable thoughts took over my spirit, plaguing me day and night.

The burial was set for the third day after death, and so, on the appointed day, the corpse was brought early to our residence, already nailed shut in the coffin, so the usual ceremony could take place from here. It pained me deeply that they had unilaterally chosen to close the coffin in the hospital, so that I could no longer see the corpse. I wanted to come along to the burial, but was told that was not customary in Hamburg. What did I care at that moment about the customs and courtesies of Hamburg! Not in the least. My pain was too intense for me to give any deference to hollow and contrived formalities. Nothing around me mattered; I was indifferent to the whole world. No one moved to order a carriage for me, and by now, little time was left to make new arrangements. I therefore decided to follow alongside the hearse on foot. But when the amiable Pastor T. heard about my desire, he kindly offered me a seat in his carriage, which I accepted with sincere thanks. And thus we commenced our sad trip, accompanied by some acquaintances.

/Although it was early August, the weather was rainy and dreary. There was not a ray of sunshine to be seen, and nature was all cloaked in grey. On this day, perhaps for the first time in my life, I did not mind forgoing the glorious, all-animating sun. Today the gloom of nature fit my mood better than a cheerful day. Allow me to skip the details of the next hour, for which words fail me. When the usual ceremonies were over, and I saw how people got ready to lower my all into the grave, I was gripped by one single wish, to belong to the caste that condemns wives to step onto the funeral pyre and thereby also follow the husband directly into death. What is the act of being burnt alive and the short suffering as compared to the constant and indescribable pain of a poor mortal soul. "These thoughts are heathen," you will surely be thinking. And so they certainly are, for they fit neither Islam, nor Christianity. Are the many torments we must undergo on this earth not much worse than a short death by fire?

I am told I gripped the coffin so vehemently that people could barely wrest me from it. Did it not contain everything I possessed?! My children? Oh yes, but at this moment, they gave me no solace. To the contrary, I even believed I could bear my misery more easily without them, as I felt so abandoned and alone. And perhaps this is exactly why I saw no comfort in my children, because without them I would have made my way from the burial grounds straight to the train and from there onward to you. And what else might have shackled me to this place? Absolutely nothing!

We started our way back home, while I sat in silence wishing the trip would never end. I simply dreaded returning to the quotidian cast of people, the house, the furniture, and such. Upon entering the house, my three children were brought to me. According to local custom, they were for the first time dressed in half-mourning, which I found to be a melancholy sight. Everything, everything in the house seemed to remind me of my loss. The house felt devoid of life, even though only one person was missing. No place gave me peace, and I wandered from one room to another as though driven by ghosts. I resented my fate and eternal providence. I felt spurned by my Creator and was thus totally unmoored. Although prayer would have been the one avenue to bring me some solace, for the first time in my life, alas, I could not do it. My soul was in a kind of revolution and now had to fight its way through. When I finally found the conviction to pray as I had, of course, been taught from youth onward: "Nothing shall ever happen to us but what the Lord has decreed for us, so praise be unto him forever, Amen!"[56], I began to feel somewhat better inside.

But the barrenness within me grew more and more intense.—

---

56 From the Koran, Surah at Tawbah 9:51.

The author's husband in Hamburg.

Also Hamburg, either 1869 or 1870.

12

All other desires in my soul shut down, except the one thought that took over: Leave, leave, go home! The longing for you ruled my whole being, all thoughts and all feelings. Even without awaiting the letter from our unforgettable Ch., I indeed believed entirely correctly that with the news of my loss, your thoughts would be one and the same: I must immediately return to you, naturally as one of yours. Without the mighty oceans of the world between us, and with confirmation that I was free from every moral duty, even if I had had to traverse the distance to you on foot, I would not have hesitated a single second to say yes.

My husband died without leaving a will, without ever having spoken even one word about the future of me and the children, much less about how to raise them. Outwardly, I was, of course, free to go wherever I wanted, since my children were still so young and not yet subject to the usual school or military requirements. I had to undergo a huge struggle within myself—one that lasted years—to come to a decision. My whole existence was attached to you and the homeland that was paradise on earth.

/But between the two now lay the memory of my husband, which I had to honor. With a bleeding heart, I renounced the prospect of a reunion and determined, in the memory of my husband, to raise his children in his country, as he surely would have wished it. I had to acknowledge for myself that if the situation had been the reverse, I certainly would have wanted my children to have an Arab upbringing. And thus, I followed simply and solely the voice of piety, regardless of all the nice concepts here like education and civilization. For still to this day, I am not a great fan of such forcibly imposed schooling, especially if it neglects the true development of the heart. I would have made the same choice whether my husband had been Chinese or Japanese, instead of German. In so saying, I simply wanted to prove to you that what I did back then was done only out of love for the deceased and no other motive. I was too much one of you to let myself be guided by any motives other than those described above.

Back then I had decided to raise my children in their father's homeland without thinking in the least about myself. If I had been more astute in my thinking, I might have concluded otherwise, since the children naturally took on the customs and habits of the land in which they grew up, while

I naturally remained an Arab through and through. On the outside, I may appear totally "à la franca," but inside, I did not change and was also not that easy to reform. Not without some apprehension, I had to admit to myself that the path I was choosing carried rather too much risk. But it is enough for me that I acted in good faith to fulfill what I believed to be my moral duty to the deceased. Now you can also understand why giving up the thought of returning to you became so unspeakably difficult for me, since that was so very much what my heart longed for.

Had I been able to foresee the dismal years that still lay ahead of me here, I doubt I would have had the necessary courage to carry out my intentions. The loneliness inside, and the boundless emptiness in the house grated unceasingly on my soul. I often just felt absent and had to exert great effort to pay attention to what was being said to me. My husband's smoking room, where I had a view of the garden and the Alster, became my constant abode. Already three weeks had passed since my hard fate had befallen me. As usual, I sat there, disconsolate in my thoughts, staring blankly ahead of me, when suddenly I jumped up and hurried to the front door to open it, as I had previously done so frequently when my husband came home. Completely crestfallen, I went back, once I realized my mistake. My young son, who was hardly one and a half years old, called for his father all day long, which always threatened to break my heart. My eldest daughter, all of two and a half years old, noticed this so much that she whispered to her little brother, do not call Papa or else Mama will cry. And then she would regularly traipse over to me with her tiny handkerchief and wipe away my tears.

In the meantime, it was October. On that day, as best I can recall, it was very damp, cold, and dreary. Around five in the afternoon, lunch was announced, and I remember going to the table. Shortly thereafter, however, I apparently got up abruptly, without having touched the food, left the house just as I was, neither coat nor hat, and headed rapidly down the street. Not until the Walhalla steamboat station did people catch up with me and bring me back home again. During this time, I suffered from severe headaches that plagued me day and night. I had this constant feeling of ants crawling under the skin of my head. The doctor thought it was the nerves on my head that caused these complaints.

In this ailing state, I received the completely devastating news that my noble brother M.[57] had died, a last blow suited to crush my soul. You know, of course, what I lost in him. I deeply mourned the loss of this kindhearted brother, who had been especially forbearing and loving toward me, who was uniquely qualified, like no other, to replace our noble and justice-seeking father. It also reflects tellingly on M.'s magnanimity that when B.[58] took the reign after him, the latter is said to have on some occasion called out to the notables in the land: "My father was your father, and M. was your brother, but I am your ruler and master!" You will recall how much bad blood these words evoked among the people.

Because of the poor postal connections between Zanzibar and Germany at the time, I had no inkling of M.'s sickness, and so the news of his passing caught me totally unprepared. This sad dispatch only served to heighten my longing for my beloved homeland. I now felt doubly disconnected, as I had not a single soul here with whom I could have discoursed at length about you all and our circumstances. Oh, you have no idea how much this sentiment oppressed me and left me feeling like a complete stranger. If the children had been even just a bit older, perhaps I would not have had to feel quite so mentally forlorn. That very headstrong Salme of but a few years ago would have been unrecognizable if you had seen her now in an unguarded hour. It is indeed remarkable how quickly humans can change under certain conditions.

/Because of the circumstances in these first months of my mourning, I became so very indifferent toward even my beloved children that neither their presence nor absence had any effect on me. The inner upheaval was so overpowering that I needed considerable time to restore my lost equilibrium, even only minimally. The worst was that I did not have sufficient confidence in my ability to achieve the path I had chosen to honor my husband. My whole being, as well as the future, seemed shrouded in an impenetrable fog. Indeed, I initially had no idea how I was supposed to find my way forward. Only my old trust in the Almighty held me upright and kept my courage, at that moment, from sinking all too much.

As we say here, misfortune rarely comes alone. This also seemed to apply in my case. Even as I was still oppressed by my mental stupor, I was confronted with the bleak news that the export business between Hamburg and Zanzibar

---

57 Referring to the author's half-brother Madjid, who became Sultan of Zanzibar in 1856, when the father died.
58 Referring to the author's half-brother Barghash, who was Sultan of Zanzibar from 1870 to his death in 1888.

was in dire straits as a consequence of the German-French war, and we could expect great losses. On top of that, my husband's agent in Zanzibar, a friend from his youth and the son of a senior pastor in Hamburg, had shown a very deficient understanding of "mine and thine," and so I had to anticipate the worst. This disloyal agent tried to enrich himself as quickly as possible at the expense of the widow and fatherless children of his deceased friend, against which the Hamburg-based liquidator of my husband's business was unable to exercise any effective control.

/Given this situation, the view was that I needed to be prepared to significantly limit my expenditures from now on, and that I would be unable to continue our previous lifestyle. This news had anything but an uplifting effect on me. Even though my soul needed no wealth, luxury, and all the rest, and was instead more than content with an average lifestyle, and could never thank the Giver of all earthly things enough for our daily bread, I could not possibly remain indifferent to these bad tidings. As such, I could not help but be reminded of our Arab saying that privation, hardship, or need is nowhere and under no circumstances felt as oppressively as in a foreign land! Yes, in a land that truly felt so very foreign to me. Oh my God, I could have been knocked to the moon or some other celestial body and my loneliness and helplessness would have been the same.

/We need a certain amount to survive everywhere in the world, but the exact quantity always depends on the location. You may have heard how expensive life is in Europe, compared to our blessed homeland. Amounts that are in excess there would cover only the most necessary items here, and perhaps not even suffice for that. You cannot imagine what kinds of sums are consumed by a decent European household. You cannot even dream how much the countless needs grow from year to year.

I was filled with anxious foreboding, for what should I do now, and where should I even begin? The first thing that needed to happen, of course, was to terminate the villa, where we had been living, and move into a cheaper residence. I also let go of the chambermaid, to whom I had gotten very accustomed, thereafter retaining only one servant girl across-the-board and one nanny. Until then, we had sent out all our loads of laundry, but now I hired a wash lady to come once a week to wash the clothes in our home, which somewhat reduced our weekly expenditures. And I decided henceforth, once and for all, not to make any purchases that I could not immediately pay in cash. Back then in Hamburg, it was customary to let all purchases accrue on credit until the new year— excluding the grocer, baker, butcher, milkman, etc. that are paid weekly. Given

The author's half-brother, Sultan Madjid.

The author's half-brother, Sultan Barghash.

my math incompetence at the time, I could hardly have kept proper track of our debits and credits any other way.

/Worst of all for me was the fact that I had absolutely no idea how much money we had and what I could afford to spend. This rather disconcerting situation unfortunately lasted more than three full years. Against this backdrop, feeling totally powerless and fully dependent on the grace and mercy of strangers, I suffered terribly. Do not ever let yourself be persuaded by the fairy tale that widows and orphans generally fare better in Europe than with you. Perhaps excluding the orphanages, which have become necessary for the enormous populations in European cities. For them, however, the people here pay immense taxes, which are unknown to you.

Never a fan of Northern winters, and always happy when summer returned, I found this winter even more unbearable than usual. The foggy, dreary weather of November and December weighed so heavily on me that I have no words to describe it. Spiritual emptiness and loneliness, plus the early darkness of the winter days, conspired to oppress me. No rays of hope anywhere, neither outside, nor within my soul. In addition, I was overcome by an inexplicable, but excruciating, sense of fear that plagued me day and night. I was often stalked by the notion that the lives of me and my children were no longer entirely safe in this alien environment after the death of my husband. I therefore rather frequently gathered my unsuspecting small children and locked myself up with them in my room for several hours.

/All these feelings and beliefs I had to keep to myself, so as not to be misunderstood or even wrongly judged. Truly, did I have anyone who could fully understand me and grasp my situation? No one, absolutely no one. To avoid revealing my weakness to the cold, indifferent world, or even making myself a laughing stock, I made sure not to show any of this to the outside. Certainly, it would have been hard for anyone without similar experiences to comprehend my state. Fortunately, there are, I believe, not many who have gotten to know the full spectrum of misery as much as I have.

/Certainly, now and again there were people who meant well with me and tried to comfort me in their way. I say, in their way, because after I once called out in utter despair: "Oh, if I knew not that this was my God's will, I could never find peace!", the response was to try to reeducate me. I was asked if I really believed that God in fact takes care of our fates and everything we encounter on this earth. I need not describe to you how innerly appalled I was at this profane question. It seems to me that but a very few, select Christians are familiar with the complete Holy Scripture, which clearly enough tells us that the Lord knows the number of our hairs and that no sparrow falls off the roof without His will.[59] On such occasions, I could not thank the Lord enough for letting me enter this world as a Muslim.

/It was always hard not to compare how little Muslims are taught about their own religion and yet exhibit such solid faith—in contrast to Christian children, who are so painstakingly instructed in school. I had the impression that religion is taught here more as mere science, to be forgotten again at the first opportunity or even oft-criticized, as I regrettably had to observe several times. How else would there be so many tragic suicides if people believed in God and his purposes! In the face of whatever misfortune, be it a death in the family, business losses, often completely unintentional slights, and many other trivial matters, people here turn straight to suicide. Yes, even half-grown youngsters, when they are expecting a well-deserved punishment at home, prefer to take their lives than face parental punishments. Would they do all this if they had even some minimal religion in their soul? Surely never!

---

59 Here the author is paraphrasing from the Bible, Matthew 10:29–30.

/13

Your warship, the *Ilmedjidi*, came to Hamburg in the most severe cold of that same winter, purportedly to be repaired. The Hamburg company to which this ship was sent was an avowed enemy of my husband, for the simplest of reasons, namely: He did business in Zanzibar as well. I had many opportunities to experience this inexcusable fault, as the widow of this deceased competitor. Of course, you know that this company flew the German, which is to say at that time the Hamburg, consular flag, which also carried the moral duty to intervene on behalf of the estates of all decedents under their protection. In my case, they completely failed their obligation. Even after I personally went to their Hamburg bureau to request support in dealing with the liquidation of my husband's business in Zanzibar, nothing happened.

/With this example, you can see how much you all were mistaken if you thought that I, having married a German and a Christian, would never lack for aid or assistance. Oh, what a fallacy! Believe me, that was nothing more than pure illusion on your parts. That an Arab would marry a German, and a Muslim would become Christian, is so inconsequential that no one pays any attention to it. You are too far away from the European arena to be able to assess the true conditions. What governs here is always the same: Every man for himself! And if you happen not to be a man, then the mere nationality of your husband will do little to help you. As far as our country and its customs more generally, the English nationality is preferable by far. Because of their experience with the Indian colonies, the English are better able to deal with Orientals, especially with Arabs.

While the *Ilmedjidi* lay in the harbor, our unforgettable M. had long since left the land of the living, and his successor had exclusive rights over the ship. As always in this world, here, too, the weak ones lose out. Back then, my own fate was keeping me busy, and I gave little thought to the ship. One day, as I headed into town along one of the main streets for an errand, I saw, from afar, at least a hundred people gathered ahead of me. Not suspecting anything, I tried to make my way through the crowd until I suddenly stood stock still in front of a group of people. What did I see? Across from me, completely unexpected, was a group of our sailors, of whom I believed to even recognize a few. My feelings cannot be described. At first, I wanted to walk over to the sailors and talk to them, but then my thoughts turned to the dear public that surrounded us and surely would have recognized me on this occasion and then treated me with the usual curiosity. And what fodder that would have been for the local section of the newspapers, naturally embellished with plenty of fantasy. Taking into account all of these factors, I decided, with much emotional tumult, to step into a coach and let myself be driven back to my home.

/If I had had any inkling of this encounter, I would have opted to stay home. My extreme longing for you all was stoked anew by this experience, and the thought that had never fully left me—leave, leave, go home!—was revived. It was only your slaves that I saw this day, and yet, the sight of them once again awakened a world of memories.

/In my current attire, there was no chance the sailors would ever recognize me, so I was safe that way. I speculated that the men would very probably ask about me and try to find me. And so it was. About two weeks after my street encounter, I was alone in my room, consumed by melancholy thoughts of the past and fearful thoughts of our future. The servant girl came in and told me that about twenty African men wanted to see me. It was not hard to guess who my guests were, and I therefore let them come in. You should have seen the scene that now followed. We had barely exchanged our Arabic greetings when the men all threw themselves at my feet, reverently kissed the floor, and broke out in hefty tears. I would be lying if I were to insist that my eyes stayed dry at this moment. How could that have been possible! Taking this all in, my traditional sense of social hierarchy disappeared, and I saw in this group only one thing, that they came from Zanzibar—and from all of you. I will tell you quite openly that a visit from a hundred strangers with crowns on their heads would not have moved me as much as the presence of these plain people. As if in unison, these men called out in Arabic: "Thanks be to the Lord our God that we found you! *O Bibi tua*! (Our Mistress!) How long we have searched for you!"

The Zanzibari warship Ilmedjidi, *here as the former Confederate raider CSS* Shenandoah

/Those were the first words of these good and simple men. Our touching reunion must have been very moving, since I found both of my German servant girls, who of course understood not a single word of what we were speaking, sobbing loudly at the door. Not all the men were African, as the servant girl had announced, but about half were Arab. Under no circumstances did they want to sit on chairs, and so they seated themselves cross-legged on my rug, just as we are used to doing at home, gathering all around me. When I asked how they had managed to find me, they told me the following:

/As soon as we arrived in Hamburg, we asked every European in English—the sailors did not understand German—that came to us on the ship to tell us where you live, but no one was willing or able to answer. Most of the fine gentlemen who came to see the *Ilmedjidi* simply shrugged their shoulders at our questions and said they did not know your whereabouts. But finally yesterday, when two of us wanted to buy some smoking tobacco, they went into a store and also tried to use this opportunity to find out your address. The tobacco salesman then said to them that he had lately seen frequent stories about me in the paper and wanted to look for my address in a big book (presumably the address book). Then he wrote something on a piece of paper, which we naturally could not read. With this paper in your hand, he told us, you will indeed find your Mistress, and so it was. These two comrades shared their experience and successful venture with us. Practically all of us wanted to come find you immediately, but not everyone could get permission. Now we want to take turns to visit you, so we can all see you.—With this slip of paper in hand, asking on the street all along the way, people finally led us to your door, for which we cannot thank the Lord enough.

Although the poor sailors were dressed in thick European outfits, the harsh winter made them so freezing cold that they were truly to be pitied. In the course of the conversation, after many greetings from home had been extended, and I, as you can surely imagine, had no shortage of questions, several of them suddenly called out: "*Bibi, unawesage kukandan ja inchi kana hiji?*" (Bibi, how can you live in such a land?) "*Tafasali rudi kuwetu, watu wote wanakutamani ssana!*" (Please come back to us, all the people are yearning for you!) These words almost broke my heart, and I could only shake my head and wistfully respond, "*ssissassa, ssissassa!*" (not now, not now!). "*Lakini lini tena, Bibi?*" (But when, Bibi?) "*Wakiwa Watoto wakuba kidodo.*" (When the children are somewhat older.)

/That I would have gladly followed their advice, I need not reaffirm for you. But the duty to the deceased to raise his children as he would have wanted and in his fatherland, to the extent possible, exerted all its power on me to keep me here.

Your reproach that I did not love you enough to leave Germany and hurry straight to you after the death of my husband, was all too cruel. Have I not, in my difficult position, unceasingly asked the dear God for help and support, since I always remained discontented inside, indeed utterly miserable. I must reiterate for you that what I did back then occurred only because I wanted to show my last love to the deceased; as to all else, I knew myself to be free of any other considerations.

From this point on until their departure, the sailors, coming mostly in smaller groups, were my daily guests. Some of them played with the children and often took them on walks. Naturally, they favored S.[60] because I had named him after my noble father. They loved to pull the extra-large stroller, built expressly to fit all three children, through the garden. On such occasions, a large group of people would usually gather in front of our yard, enough to constitute a crowd. I had them served coffee in the usual European cups, since I no longer had enough of the little Arab ones, and they apparently found it very strange to find that missing in my house. They called the Occidental coffee cups simply "*bakuli kuba*" (big *Kummen*[61] or even bowls). The first time I had them served something to eat, they long hesitated to enjoy what had been offered, and I had to repeatedly urge them to dig in or the food would very soon get cold. To which one of the Arabs asked a question that surely was not easy for him to ask: "Bibi, the servant girl has not put pork in the food, that is true, is it not?" Only after I had clearly assured them that they could, in my house, at all times, rest easy on this point, did they decide to partake.

/Often enough I had to act as their paymaster as well because I, as they said, was not only their Bibi, but also their father, mother, and sole relative in Hamburg. Some of them implored me almost daily to let them stay and take care of the children until we could travel back together. That I would have loved only too much to keep them here, you can surely imagine. But to want and to be able are obviously two very different things, and only the most privileged mortals can master both at once. Coming exactly at this moment, when circumstances were forcing me to let one servant girl go and generally scale back my lifestyle, this request felt like an irony of fate, these people suggesting unawares that I should keep several of them with me as servants. To educate them on this point would have been futile, since they would have had no sense for, much less any understanding of, the high cost of living in Europe, especially Hamburg, in comparison to our plentiful island.

---

60 S. refers to the author's son and middle child, who was born Rudolph Said Ruete. He later changed his name to Rudolph Said-Ruete (last name hypenated) when, in 1906, the city of Hamburg finally granted his request to preserve his Sultan grandfather's name as part of his last name (perhaps corresponding to the customary Arabic "bin Said").

61 A regional German word used by the author for cups.

/As the time drew near for the *Ilmedjidi* to return home, and the ones who absolutely wanted to stay with me shared their serious intent to desert their posts, I considered it my duty to notify the ship commander with enough time for him to keep the sailors on board. As you know, the *Ilmedjidi*, together with its entire crew, totally foundered a few years later. These poor people!

The author's father, Sayyid Said bin Sultan.

/14

The following spring my children and I moved into a different, cheap and simple, residence. Because the new home was much smaller than the villa we had been living in, it was with a heavy heart that I had to sell some of the furniture. Leaving our old home hit me very hard, oh so hard, in a way I cannot even explain. Not only was I bound to this house by countless memories that exacerbated my departure, in whose walls I had experienced both fortune and tragic misfortune, but I also had to fight another feeling. With this move, I also felt, for the first time in my life, the stinging sense of an initial descent into poverty. This change had, however, become so necessary that I could no longer, in good conscience, postpone the inevitable. Without any idea of what it takes to be a competent *Hausfrau* here, I did my best within my ability to live as economically as possible. Numb to everything else, I lived exclusively for the rapidly, oh so rapidly vanished past and for the care of my children.

With my spirit in upheaval, and feeling helpless and defenseless, it made me so happy back then when I now and again received news from you. M.[62] wrote me a heartfelt letter with the urgent plea that I should take the trip home with my children at the first opportunity. All would be good again, once I resolved to return, etc., etc. This awareness, that you had my back, gave me huge joy, and I would very often say to myself that if, over time, my self-imposed goal indeed proved too difficult a task for my strength, I would in any case return back home. But until then, I would spare nothing to try to finish what I had begun.

/This refusal, as you well know, brought upon me the unrelenting anger of B., and he never chose to forgive me until his dying day. All subsequent efforts to have him pay out even just a small portion of my inheritance were categorically rejected.[63] This much became clear to me over time, that had I been an English subject, I would have come out much better. B. was completely in English hands and had to do whatever the English required. And so, inherently, he had greater sympathy for England than any other country. Later, it was, in fact, his greatest wish to put Zanzibar under English protection, except that support from the relevant English circles was lacking at the time, so nothing changed. My English friends had advised me urgently to change my residence from

---

62 Of unknown identity, although possibly the author's half-sister Meje (*Memoirs*, p. 199) or, as Professor van Donzel speculates, the author's half-sister Mettle. E. van Donzel, p. 465.

63 The usual approach was for all living siblings to receive portions of a deceased sibling's estate. The author maintained that she had a right to this inheritance, despite her status as an infidel after her conversion to Christianity and marriage to a Christian in 1867.

Germany to England in 1875,[64] which, for all the reasons you know, reasons that of course also kept me from you, I could not do.

/Did I make the right choice in this regard? I must admit openly to you that I have asked myself this question so many times. Overall, I believe I handled the situation far too idealistically. Every year more than a hundred thousand people leave Germany, some to become American subjects, some English. And these are even full-blooded Germans, meaning pure Germans, more German than my children. From a purely materialistic point of view, I did not approach things carefully enough back then, and instead gave exaggerated importance to ideals that I pursued with such effort and the greatest sacrifice.

It is its own special exercise to have to shift from living in a place where everything shortly before appeared practically in excess to suddenly being subjected to the greatest limitations. Not that I would have been enamored of all the trifles and glitter that are just for show—no, that fortunately was not my style. But the need to anxiously guard this vile Mammon, to make sure we had enough of it, was for me so oppressive and at the same time so humiliating that I can hardly describe it to you. The deck was especially stacked against me because Hamburg, of all places, turns almost exclusively on the role of money, and it was here of all places that my lucky boat ran aground. All too frequently, I was cuttingly reminded of my dismal situation.

/That I would, in keeping with my intentions, prefer to allow my children to grow up in their father's hometown is, of course, natural, even though the climate of this foggy town was hardly to my liking. But the present circumstances dictated that I begin a completely new life, to meet the new conditions, if I wanted to find enough room under a blanket that had shrunk too short. It was clear that I could not easily follow through on this in Hamburg. From our youngest days, we are accustomed to showing true humility before the Highest, indeed, we are effectively raised in it. And even so, there is nothing my people are more sensitive about than being humiliated.

/Yet, the totally different life I was going to have to live was one I had never even dreamt of. In the past, whenever I had undertaken something here or there in the household simply to pass the time, or engaged with the children too much, I was sure to hear reproaches from my dear husband, who never liked to see me working. He was always saying: "Bibi, you are not supposed

---

64 This was the year the author went to London to try to see Sultan Barghash during his State visit (*Memoirs*, pp. 205–10). Professor van Donzel also gives this as the year the author began writing her *Memoirs*, which were then published in 1886. E. van Donzel, p. 1.

to work!" Or also: "Do not always carry the children on your arm, take a seat instead, we have enough people to take care of the children!" And the like. Oh, what would he have said, if he had seen me a couple of years later in the ice-cold winter without any help at all, doing everything, yes, everything by myself, often spending half an hour beside the cold oven, bitter tears streaming down my face, before I was finally able to get the fire burning! And meanwhile, two of my children lay ill with serious cases of scarlet fever. If my husband had gone bankrupt in his lifetime, and we had lost everything that way, I would most certainly have been at his side to perform the most difficult and, if needed, also most demeaning work for him and the children.

/The thought of continuing to live in this, for me, so incredibly complicated European setting, and the memory of my irreplaceable loss, often robbed me of my courage to go on. Above all, I was pursued by a constant feeling of abandonment that threatened to break my heart throughout every day. Under these circumstances, everything became so very difficult for me, and over time, I started to lose my resolve. "Strength, oh Lord, strength and steadfast perseverance!" remained my constant prayer for years.

/Alone the fact that I, nonetheless, managed to keep all five of my senses shows the great mercy of the Lord. I can tell you openly that I was close to losing my mind. The doctor wanted me to go out frequently, to get more movement. My headaches became increasingly severe, and the feeling that thousands of ants were crawling under the skin of my head made me very nervous. No medication proved helpful. And taking aimless walks, always completely alone because my children were still much too young to join me, was truly dreadful. I therefore decided, in order to follow the doctor's orders, to take lessons from a writing teacher far off in the city, so I would have a practical destination for my outings. Twice a week, rain or shine, I would go there and back by foot, from Blücherstrasse up to near the Thalia Theatre,[65] where the teacher lived.

In the meantime, I was seriously considering leaving Hamburg in the not-too-distant future and seeking another cheaper residence, as it became increasingly clear that staying in Hamburg was out of the question in the long run. Or should I first wait for my children to go to school, where they would be confronted with all the other children that were raised in luxury in this city and then feel disadvantaged by fate? No, I hoped to spare them and myself precisely that. But where should I point my feet to find what I was looking for? That constituted a serious problem for me.

---

65 About an hour's walk each way. According to meticulous research by Fridjof Gutendorf, she was headed to J.G. Herbst's lessons in "Schön- und Schnellschreiben" at Raboisen 74.

/My deliberations were met with very little understanding within the narrow circles I frequented, which left me feeling quite uncomfortable. Once again, I had to deal with strangers who somehow imagine they can better ascertain other people's circumstances, yes, even their feelings and perceptions, than the people themselves. I was cited hundreds of examples of other women and widows who were able to live their lives in Hamburg with even more limited means than mine, and more of the same. But such lecturers apparently did not get that these women and widows were Hamburg born and bred, for whom it would be natural to stay in their homeland, whereby I, in contrast, as a non-German, with nothing to anchor me to Hamburg, could just as well choose to take up residence anywhere. It also seemed to me, over and over again, that most people, despite having written the word "freedom" on their flags, are hardly inclined to give others the same degree of freedom. It is, above all, rather rare to find that people are treated on an individual basis, rather than generically, across-the-board, as is so often the case.

Finally, I found an unbiased lady, who came from Middle Germany and advised me to travel to Darmstadt, to have a look at that town. If I liked it, I could readily move there, since the climate would be somewhat warmer and the cost of living somewhat cheaper than here in Hamburg. My decision to travel there without another living soul and spend time there with complete strangers did not come easily. And yet, I had no choice but to strike out on my own, no matter the personal cost to me. Or was I to simply sit passively by and watch our pecuniary circumstances continue to go downhill, thus exposing myself to countless disagreeable experiences that could hardly be avoided and would be far harder to bear than might first appear? No, that would have been completely contrary to my nature. And so, I pulled myself together and set a date for my trip to Darmstadt.

/The train I planned to take left at six in the morning, so I ordered a coach to take me there at five, in view of the distance to the station. By the time the clock showed quarter after five, however, and the coach was still nowhere to be seen, the servant girl and I hoisted the leather suitcase and travel bag and headed to the home of the driver in question, who lived not all too far from us. Upon arrival, I was very surprised to find everything deathly quiet and the driver still needing to be awakened from his deep sleep. After much loud calling, he finally came to the window, only half awake and in his shirt sleeves. At which point, as later recounted by my servant girl, I apparently called to the driver, "Mr. Hinrichs, should I help you dress the horse?" Oh, what did I know about terms like harnessing and hitching, as they refer to it here.

/The courtyard where the coach stood, was set back quite some distance, a good stretch from the road. While the driver began to put on the driving harness with the help of the servant girl, I started pulling the coach toward the street all by myself, in an effort to expedite our already extremely late trip to the train. It really was high time for us to get going, and then we rode wildly toward the station. Once arrived, the guileless Hinrich called after me multiple times: "Hurry, Madam, if you still want to catch the train!" As if pursued, I dashed to the box office, got my ticket, and then half-ran all the way to the car. Barely had I set my foot in the door than the train was in motion.

/As I sat, still completely drained from this unaccustomed mad dash, my environment mercilessly confronted me with the reality of my life. The bare walls, the unupholstered seats, stared me in the face with such pity, such questions, that I broke down and erupted in hot tears. For a long time already, I had felt my strength ebbing, yet had no choice under the given circumstances but to undertake the trip, despite the terrible headaches, which had been plaguing me for more than a year. For the first time in my life, I found myself in a third-class carriage. Fortunately, I sat alone and unobserved in the railcar and could give my emotions free rein.

/This was one of the many bitter pills I was often made to swallow. I of course had to live frugally to make ends meet. Nevertheless, there were people who called themselves "friends" who felt the need to weigh in on every little purchase I made. For example, when I had to start wearing a pince-nez, as prescribed by the eye doctor to address the stress on my eyes, I undertook something completely unacceptable by procuring one with a golden rim, for which my "friends" resented me. On this occasion, I first learned the meaning of the local saying: "Lord, protect me from my friends, for I can handle my enemies on my own!"

/I took the third-class ticket this time, traveling on my own, to carry the humility alone and then planned to take my children along only once I had withstood this trial. Even though my children were still so young that they had no real grasp of life, much less the different train compartments, I did not want to expose them right away to the ugly third class. Such are the cares of a mother, who had to learn step-by-step that she would have to bow deeply in order not to break.

The trip took quite a while, and it was already late when the train arrived in Darmstadt. I had a driver take me to a simple hotel, where I stayed in my room until the next morning. I then got up early to quickly gather information about housing, grocery prices, and similar aspects, without which I would have had no real basis for comparison. The caretaker of the hotel was my only source of information, since I knew no one in the area. However, this unsophisticated attendant treated me with totally blatant curiosity, no doubt unaccustomed to encountering someone like my lowly self, born near the Equator and a relatively brown complexion. Instead of answering my questions, as much as I cared about getting answers, she took it upon herself to interrogate me, like, for example, what country I came from (here I used a white lie and named a South American region in response), and if I also had a husband and children. When I responded that I was a widow with small children, she started to take pity on me. Following her advice, I took a coach to see some of the housing. But, how unfortunate! Everywhere the same questions: Where are you from, my lady, do you have acquaintances here who can vouch for you, and so on. Not a very encouraging welcome for a stranger, to be sure. These and similar questions were so disheartening for my already alienated and downtrodden soul that I gave up the idea of moving to the area and accordingly embarked on my return to Hamburg the very next morning.

/This type of mistrust against anyone who was not a full-blooded German is something I subsequently came across many times in Germany. And I was often forced to consider how offensive it must be for someone to be confronted with such mistrust right from the start (as my case in Darmstadt had sufficiently demonstrated). Later, a Hungarian woman in Dresden complained about the exact same treatment, and likewise a Russian woman. How so very different it is for you, where every European, if there was no reason to think otherwise, is accorded complete trust, whether this person was an upstanding citizen or a crook in his homeland. It is just too unkind to give non-Germans such dubious treatment when there is no reason to be wary of them.

I arrived back in Hamburg rather disappointed. On the return, I remembered a lady, who had told me much about Dresden, where she lived, when I had made her brief acquaintance. I decided to turn to this woman and inquire further about the conditions there. I wrote the letter myself, although do not ask me how. In any case, the sweet lady managed to decipher my letter, for she answered my various questions in great detail. Thereupon I decided to travel to Dresden myself, potentially to rent a place while there. I had the impression that life in Dresden was significantly less expensive than in Hamburg. I also hoped to live as peacefully and reclusively as possible, so that I might devote myself entirely to the care of my children.

/Dresden immediately made a good impression on me, also helped by the fact that the family of this lady (an officer's family from Hanover) gave me the warmest welcome. Thus the two of us, my new friend and I, went apartment hunting. Up the stairs, down the stairs, fortunately we were both still young, or we might not have had the stamina. Since this friend was a very determined lady and did not readily take an X for a Y, I hardly had to talk to any of the many landlords myself. I was indeed grateful not to have to listen to the insipid questioning again this time: Where do you come from, my lady? and all that. If my German had been any better at the time, I would have gladly told those good people in Darmstadt: I am from the moon, dear folks! The people in the interior of Germany back then had as little sense of Zanzibar as you to this day have of Siberia and the endless snowfields. It would have taken an extended discourse to educate them about the existence of our dear island, and even then, I doubt they would have believed me. I have often been reminded of our very apt saying, roughly translated as "Those who do not know you also cannot assess you."[66]

A little house with a bit of garden, to live separately as I would have preferred, was not to be found at a price I could afford. On the other hand, the thought of living in a big house on one floor together with other people was extremely unpleasant for me, so that I entertained my companion's very practical suggestions only with reluctance. One of the options was for me to rent the attractive ground floor on ____ Street that was too expensive for me, but then rent out a few furnished rooms. At first, I found the idea thoroughly appalling. From now on, I would not only have to live like a bird in a cage on a single floor, but also need to rent out a few rooms to offset the high rent, if I wanted a spacious home in a healthy location. I had come to Dresden at a very inopportune time, since it was after the usual period when apartments change hands, and it was not easy to find something fitting. I ultimately chose the place on ____ Street after all, with the intention of subletting two furnished rooms, and then traveled back to Hamburg to arrange the move.

/The relocation of a well-equipped European household by train is one of the most unpleasant things, one that you would be hard-pressed to imagine, if only because you do not even know the names of the many useful and less-than-useful items. Your home arrangements that have continued unchanged for hundreds of years are no grounds for comparison, in that here every generation has its own very specific fashion and taste. We often see how the parents and grandparents are satisfied with basic furnishings, while their offspring want

---

66 *Asiyejua kitu, hawezi kujua thamani yake*, translated as "A person who does not know an object cannot know its value," according to "Swahili Proverbs: Methali Za Kiswahili," posted by the Center for African Studies at the University of Illinois at Champaign-Urbana.

only the absolute newest and ever more elegant things. Our household was not overdone, but still expansive enough for me to have to consider whether all these things were truly necessary. The packing of the furniture proceeded, and about two weeks later, we, my children, a nanny and I, sat in the train on the way to the capital of Saxony.

During these last days in Hamburg, I frequently visited my dear gravesite, as the only place where my soul could confess all its suffering. Is it just an illusion when the losses we suffer make us feel even more strongly that our loved ones only give the appearance of being dead, and that they instead are as aware of all our earthly woes as we are? Oh, can anyone unravel this puzzle other than the Almighty alone?! Regardless, this idea gave me great comfort in my bereavement.

15

In Germany, France, and most other European countries, custom requires that newcomers make the first visits after their arrival. In addition, anyone who leaves must make farewell visits, just the opposite of what we are used to. In this regard, the English are an exception, in that they visit the new arrivals first, just as we do. They reason that it is kinder to welcome unfamiliar strangers to new locations and help them, if possible. But, if I did not want to come across as too backwards, I had to make the rounds of all the Hamburg ladies who were my friends and acquaintances to take my leave. More limited is the practice of giving gifts to someone who is departing, if only a trifle, as a sign of love; only true Orientals still engage in this custom.

It is only too understandable that I could not leave a city, in which I had spent the bleakest hours of my life, without inner agitation.

Steel engraving of Dresden, mid-1800s.

16

As fate would have it, my landlady in Dresden turned out to be from Hamburg and had, as she said, already heard much about me. I was therefore spared the question: "Where do you come from?" On the second day of our move, when everything on our floor still lay in complete disarray, and I had on a large working apron while helping the movers with the unpacking and arranging—as the servant girl had the difficult task of keeping my three young and very lively children away from the chaos in the apartment—I received an invitation from my landlady to a coffee. I was invited at three o' clock and was supposed to go down at four, as my landlady lived on the ground floor, while I was one floor up. I would have much preferred to decline the invitation, since I was more than occupied, but went anyhow, so as not to insult anyone. Who can describe my surprise when I arrived and did not see the lady of the house anywhere, even after the coffee was carried in, but rather found myself alone with the man of the house.

/Although providence in no way determined to make me a shy person—a trait that would not have let me overcome all the steep and anything but rose-bestrewn paths of my life—I nonetheless felt quite ill at ease sitting together with a completely unknown gentleman. But the riddle was soon solved, for I had taken but a few sips of the rather weak coffee when my counterpart began to clear his throat and said approximately the following to me: "Madam, tomorrow I am traveling to the trade fair in Leipzig, ahem, ahem—and I am in need of funds, so may I not receive the rent from you immediately?"—"Yes, certainly, Mr. X, with the whole move, I overlooked the need to get the rent to you in advance, please accept my apology." A quarter hour later, I sent the money down with my servant girl, who soon returned with the receipt. Just as I had thought, it was in fact, for I later found out that the wife had kept her distance, so as not to be witness to her husband—nota bene, the happy owner of more than a million—when he admonished me about the rent. Had this rich landlord considered that the rent I just paid constituted nearly all of my cash? Hardly! But so it was, and that only increased my motivation to get the apartment in place as quickly as possible, so I could rent out the two furnished rooms. Soon I succeeded in finding a couple, which had lived in Brazil many years and had a black servant, that wanted the rental for two months.

/Who was happier on this day than I! For let me tell you that worries about one's daily bread bear down on everything and crush the courage to live. What that means—N.B. for a miserable Arab woman, such as myself—to care for children and household, often without knowing where the small sums needed for the next day should come from, can be understood only by someone who has been in the same situation as I have. And all that because widows and orphans here are especially cared for.

/After the death of my husband, I was designated the sole heir, namely for so long as I stayed a widow and did not remarry. This was determined according to Hamburg law, under which my assets were not divided between me and my children. The court named me the guardian of my children—without my fully suspecting or understanding what that in fact involved—along with the additional caveat that I was strictly obligated to designate two men as my "assistants." Until then, the word assistant was completely unknown to me, much less any inkling of what this position and its related duties entailed. So I had to ask what was meant by this term and how I was expected to behave towards them. Whether I understood or not did not trouble the court. The fact that I had been born in faraway Africa, and not on the shores of the Elbe, or that I had little sense of European ways, appeared to be outside the concern of the law.

/I asked two gentlemen from my circle to take on this position of assistant, which they did. They proceeded to invest my money in Russian and American bonds, Hungarian railway stocks, and mortgages. The concept of bonds and railway stocks was completely alien to me back then, and it took a long time before I could understand and appreciate their nature. Shortly before my move to Dresden, both gentlemen resigned from their positions, which left me having to find two others. One was our reliable, older house doctor, whom I had come to appreciate highly; the other was a very well-known lawyer. The house doctor accepted the position only nominally because, as he explained, he did not much understand these things and also had a very demanding practice. That left me to deal solely with the lawyer when it came to financial matters.

/It turned out this lawyer was entirely capricious and unaccountable in his treatment of my affairs, often causing me to suffer to the point of destitution. Even after three years of being a widow, I still had no idea how much yearly interest was at my disposal! It took great effort and multiple admonitions before I got my regular allowance, and then he would again leave me without a penny, no matter how much I pleaded. As a result, my daily life became so indescribably difficult. I was left completely in the dark and all my queries remained unanswered, such that I had no idea how much annual budget I had available.

/Under all this extreme duress, I survived many a day with barely a thaler in my possession. Of course, I could have borrowed some money to manage my immediate needs and feed my children something other than exclusively soup meat, while contenting myself with a dry slice of dark bread and a glass of milk to still my evening hunger. I always hated borrowing, and so I could not, even in the direst of circumstances, allow this evil enemy to enter my life.

/Dismal, such dismal times were upon me, and I had to rally all my remaining strength to avoid succumbing to the bitter hours of my life. Even the children's little piggybank had to give up its contents of crown thalers, so we could procure the absolute essentials. And when once again all the pleading and admonishing to this Mr. Assistant that he send some funds remained unanswered, and the few thalers in the piggybank had been used up, there I stood one day without any cash available at all. Picture my situation when the servant girl came to me as usual to get the money for the market, which was cheaper than the store—and I simply had no penny. In my thoughts, I had long seen this day coming and also considered the necessary recourse. But the prospect of this very step weighed on me more and more, from one day to the next, until finally I could no longer evade it. I was, in fact, thinking of selling my jewelry, so I could confront the penury staring me in the face. And yet, I held onto these things tightly, out of piety for the days gone by, while dreading the inevitable trip to the jeweler.

/I told the servant girl that I had no small bills or coins in the house, but would bring some with me upon returning from the city. All I said was true, except I withheld that I not only had no small bills—but actually none. Then I opened my cabinet and took out a pair of earrings that you know from before, which I had had adjusted at the start of my stay in Hamburg. I quickly deposited the earrings in my purse when I heard the steps of my children coming to the door, inseparable from me as always, since I simply shied away from their innocent questions. Despite their youth, they were extraordinarily alert and sharply observant. Indeed, how could I have answered their query: "Mother dear, what are you going to do with those earrings?" I had no courage to tell them the bitter truth, but they were also not used to hearing me spout some other kind of story.

/And thus I went with a troubled heart to a jeweler in the old part of the city. It seemed like I had stolen the earrings from someone, rather than being their rightful owner, and I felt so insecure along the way, as though I had committed a crime. I stood in front of the jeweler's expensive shop window for a long time before being able to take heart and go in. Finally, I stepped inside, and a young, somewhat Jewish-looking gentleman, dressed in the latest fashion, bowed to me and asked in French what had brought me here. Timidly, I pulled out my little box and asked him in German if he wanted to purchase the earrings. In this moment, my existence seemed so miserable and worthless that I would have welcomed a sudden death for me and my children as the best recourse for this wretchedness. I do not wish to say much about the haggling and depreciating valuations of the jeweler, except that I finally succeeded after endless efforts to sell the earrings for an amount far under their actual value and then rushed home with the proceeds to my children ....

/I remember very well that I was unable to eat anything that day. We say back home that the cow worshippers, the Banyans, are the worst cutthroats. That may be true, but they are not the only ones, for people like that can be found everywhere and surely not least in Europe. Much later, I had a similar experience, which was unfortunately even far less heartening. You will probably remember that golden clasp, which I had commissioned out of solid gold and modeled to look like the English Marines. When it came time to dispose of this piece as well, I took it to a famous jeweler and asked him to give me an estimate, as I wanted to sell it. The gentleman in question gave me an amused look of pity, since he evidently saw me as naïve and confused. Without giving the clasp any attention, he gave it back to me and said very kindly: "We only work with gold and silver!" I did not, however, allow this to put me off, but rather told him he should please make the effort to test the clasp on a touchstone. On the inside, I was indignant that this person could believe I had brought in a worthless item, perhaps of brass, when the clasp in fact consisted of eighteen carat gold. The unerring stone thus proved the correctness of my assertion and revealed the jeweler's mistrust as completely without basis. Slowly and guardedly, he had to admit that the solid wrought clasp was indeed eighteen carat gold. And then it was time for the usual perceptive questioning: "You are in fact a foreigner, not a German, are you not?" "Well, do I look German?" I retorted, whereupon the jeweler simply answered no. Having been rather irritated by the jeweler's behavior, I started to wrap up the clasp and said to him: "If you knew I was a foreigner and not a German, why did you ask?" I then went into a simpler shop, where I sold the clasp by the weight of the gold and fewer words. Later I learned that the same was converted to coinage in the mint. Who knows if it may not someday find its way back to you as coins!

The extra room rental unfortunately did not work out well, since our place lay rather far from the city that foreigners tended to prefer. I soon had to accept that I could no longer stay on this expensive floor. When my one-year contract came to an end, we transferred to another cheaper residence. Before I moved out, however, the landlady visited me to invite me to coffee the following day. I told her that if she was planning to invite other guests as well, I would thank her but decline the kind invitation, as I preferred to avoid social gatherings. However, if the invitation was only with her, I would gladly come. She confessed, not without some embarrassment, that another older lady, the Baroness von Such-and-Such,[67] would also be present, having expressed the wish to make my acquaintance and asked my landlady to facilitate the encounter. Whereupon I declined even more decisively with the explanation that I did not enjoy meeting such inquisitive people, in addition to not wishing to make any new acquaintances. My landlady then launched into such begging and pleading that I not disappoint this honorable lady of high standing, who although a stranger had a fondness for me. You know, of course, that I have always appreciated older people and hold them in some degree of piety. With this in mind, I finally let my landlady persuade me and agreed to the visit.

/When I arrived the next day at the appointed time, the guest in question was already there. We were introduced to each other, and after the usual empty formalities of a first encounter, I felt myself very drawn to this older lady. She was so motherly and heartwarming that I felt an immediate, soothing effect. There was not a trace of the vulgar curiosity that I so often had to endure, just the calming presence of a motherly friend. What had started as an unwelcome meeting soon revealed itself as one of the happiest hours I have ever experienced in Germany. As I extended my hand to say farewell to this honorable old lady, who could easily have been my grandmother, I was as yet unaware that the good Lord was mercifully offering me this stranger as a moral support for my inner isolation. A few weeks later, I was very surprised by a visit from the lady in question, something I had not anticipated after my landlady had explained that she was unable to climb stairs. It was indeed touching to see how she tried to ascend them with the help of a cane. I could see how happy she was with my children, in whom she also subsequently found great pleasure. Upon departing, I led her by the arm down the stairs. When saying good-bye, she looked me straight in the eye and said: "My dear, I think we understand each other!" Oh yes, we did indeed have an understanding between us. From then on, I felt a gradual improvement in my state of mind.

/Through my new motherly friend, I was able to find the first true Christian, someone I had been seeking, unfortunately without success, all this time. Noble in her very being and devout through and through, she possessed a clear mind, which helped her see everything in sharp relief, while also allowing her to judge fairly and objectively. From then on, she called me "my precious dear" and that is how I soon felt about her. Still today and surely until the end of my life, I will bless the hour that I first saw her. She understood everything

---

67 Louise Friederike Ottilie Freifrau von Tettau, according to H. Schneppen, *Briefe,* p. 159, n. 34.

about me, as only a devoted mother can understand her child. I soon had such confidence in her that my thoughts and actions were like an open book before her.

/Oh, how often did my heavy heart lead me to her, since I could always be sure of her empathy and understanding. How often, oh how often, did I return home after being comforted and strengthened by her, able to continue the terribly difficult road in life. I could not thank the merciful Lord enough for his care. My path was truly too steep for me, and the ever-increasing barriers often threatened to block my way. The unquenchable longing for my beloved homeland that stirred in me was overpowering. Although my motherly friend and I were so far apart in age, we were nonetheless so unified in our thinking and feeling that I could always count on her being fully there for me. Quite frequently, I would sit on a stool next to her, at her request, and taking my head between her hands, she would caress me like a loving mother. "You are like a transplanted palm," she once said to me, "which, instead of being nurtured in a warm and well-kept greenhouse, has to freeze outdoors in the wind and weather. But do not give up, my precious dear, and stay confident that the Lord will be there for you." Such words of comfort did wonders for my soul, especially since my assistant, the lawyer, left much to be desired in the administration of my finances, and I went from one worry to another.

It was around fall in the second year of my time in Dresden, as I was playing with the children in the small arbor that belonged to our floor, when two elegantly attired gentlemen addressed me along the following lines: "Excuse us, does the Princess of Zanzibar perhaps live here?" And when I responded, I was the one and what could I do for them, the older of the two explained that they were planning to travel to Zanzibar, as lawyers, and would be happy to convey any message to you all. Both men appeared so mysterious to me that I thanked them for the offer, with unmistakable brevity. These same purported lawyers then wanted to speak to me again the next morning, but I let them know through my servant girl that I did not receive gentlemen who did not come recommended to me by acquaintances. What do you make of that?

My normally healthy constitution gradually began to give way, and over time, I became so nervous and irritable that my doctor prescribed a change of air as soon as possible. This was easier said than done. To take such a trip with three little children in the middle of winter to southern Europe, where everything was so expensive, went beyond my means. I had no choice but to simply stay at home. Even the smallest noise caused me to start, such that the children and servant girl always had to wear felt slippers around the house. My health the following winter left much to be desired as well, and so I had to come up with a way to spend the summer away from Dresden. I considered renting my furnished residence as a whole during the summer months, perhaps to a family that wanted to spend the summer in the city. With the countless boarding houses and furnished rooms in Dresden, there was hardly any prospect of realizing my plan. But before I simply gave up and accepted the inevitable, I wanted to try everything I could. I advertised numerous times in the papers, unfortunately to no avail. Finally, I went to a real estate agent in Victoria Street and had my residence noted just in case someone came along. Not long after, I was happily able to rent the whole floor to a Romanian princess with her children, who were planning to spend the summer in Dresden.

/This way I was now able to travel with the children to the Sächsische Schweiz.[68] Here I got to know a professor, to whom I later became much indebted. One day, the nanny brought me two calling cards: one from a lady of Russian nobility, whom I had briefly gotten to know in Dresden and who was now asking me to please assist the professor, and the second from the professor himself, who was waiting outside. I hardly wanted to believe the girl when she told me that the gentleman in question had arrived in tails, top hat, white tie, and white gloves. This ceremonious outfit surely could not have been easy for this famous academic, since I learned later through a closer acquaintance that he abhorred such formalities, and even more considering he had taken the train the whole way from Dresden.

/The purpose of his visit was to ask if I might help decipher a celestial globe, which, if I am not mistaken, was said to be more than six hundred years old. The script on the globe was in old Kufic characters,[69] with which I had only

---

68 The "Switzerland" of Saxony, a German national park southeast of Dresden that features a sandstone mountain range with stunning rock formations.
69 Kufic script, developed in Al-Kufa in Iraq, is one of the earliest handwriting styles used to record the Koran. Its calligraphic style accentuates short vertical and elongated horizontal strokes that are well-suited for inscriptions.

little familiarity. I openly admitted my lack of knowledge about this type of script that deviated significantly from ours, but let him know I was happy to try to help him in any way I could. He asked if he might return the following week, and I agreed. When he arrived the next time in the same formal attire, I considered it necessary to free him from such superfluous convention and told him: "Please, Professor, from now on come in your usual clothes." Usefully, this also allowed me to gain some knowledge about astronomy, since I had until then still relied on our understanding that the sun turns around the earth, not the other way around. That said, this dear scholar had to exert great effort to convince me of this, since our perspective made more sense to me.

/Later, after we were done deciphering and translating the text on the globe, the professor made me an extraordinarily welcome proposal, which I immediately accepted: I should give him Arabic lessons in exchange for science lessons from him. Thereafter he visited me in Dresden twice a week for us to teach each other. Such a good man! I must have handed him quite a chore to introduce me to the mysteries of science, for I did not simply accept whatever he taught me. Instead, I constantly had questions about how this or that came to be and always wanted proof. I could not have asked for a better teacher, and if I did not learn more, that was not his fault. Often I would point out that it was getting late and we should start the Arabic lesson, since he would get so caught up in his eagerness to teach me that the Arabic got short shrift. He then often answered: "No, no, your questions interest me too much, since you are like a jungle that must first be plowed to produce the lushest vegetation." From then on, I was able to read German books and papers with more understanding, and even attend scientific lectures now and again. Soon he introduced me to his wife and daughter, and I could be truly happy about their harmonious family life. And when I traveled to England, what an effort he made to teach me English history.

I must once again return to my assistant, the lawyer in Hamburg, to report on his unscrupulous behavior, which continued to cause me abject poverty. Because the wonderful jurisprudence of the City of Hamburg required that our entire capital had to reside in his hands, I was completely powerless and entirely subject to his mercy. After untold efforts, I would now and again get some money from him, but always much less than the interest accrued from our capital. I could never get him to provide an accounting, since he was always making one excuse after another, forever leaving me in the lurch. As a result, I had to resort to my jewelry far too often, as my one and only refuge, and one piece followed the next.

/One day, when it was winter and I was already in a very melancholy mood because of the dreary weather, I received a letter from a friend in Hamburg, who informed me that, as widely known in the city, the financial situation of my assistant, the lawyer, was very bad. In addition, he was said to be very dangerously sick at this moment, and the letter went on to say that if he were to die now, chances were that my children and I would just be reduced to beggars. You cannot fathom my situation then, what fate was handing me. Shocked to the highest degree by this alarming news, I stood there helpless. What should I do to avoid this looming peril? As the widow of a Hamburg citizen, I had no choice but to subordinate myself to the local laws, which is to say that as long as I did not remarry, my husband's estate and its administration remained with me. But the effective power had been put in the hands of judicially-ordered assistants, as amply demonstrated by this case. A few months before receiving the warning, I had been in Hamburg on a visit. When I asked the lawyer where he kept our papers, I received the laconic answer: "Madam, that depends entirely, for sometimes they are with a banker, sometimes they are with me." From this, it is evident that the law leaves the management of widow and orphan funds in the full and unlimited discretion of the relevant assistant.

/In my plight, I sought out the professor mentioned earlier, who gave me the good advice to turn directly to the Royal Saxon Court Office, Department of Guardianship Matters, with the request (now that I lived in Dresden) that they take up the administration of my assets. I was immediately informed that the Guardianship Office only managed money for guardianship purposes, meaning that if my application were to be accepted, it would first necessitate a division of capital between me and my children. Did I want that? Oh yes, I did want that; it was only for the children that I sought to salvage whatever could still be salvaged. My own person was the least of my thoughts. Beyond anything else, I was focused on the future of my children. Physically and mentally, I was so rundown that, more than anything, I increasingly expected my own early demise.

/The Court Office in Dresden took up my application and straightaway engaged in the necessary steps to have the Hamburg Guardianship Agency transfer our assets to the Dresden Court Office without delay. In this unsettled time, I was beset with worry and sleepless nights, and I had to take significant amounts of chloral,[70] as prescribed by the doctor, to engineer any sleep. Moreover, one of the children suffered from a perpetual throat infection, one of the bad sicknesses that holds sway in the North and made me ever fearful. You have no idea how depressing a sick room here looks in the winter. Windows and doors are shut, and felt and moss are even used to seal the windows. Meanwhile, the dense fog acts so oppressively on temperaments that there is room for nothing more than melancholic thoughts. How often, oh how often did my thoughts then fly over to our dear island, and I envied you for the constant blue sky and your simple lifestyle, which is still free of all the complications that people here characterize as achievements of civilization and emblems of the harried human spirit.

It soon became clear that my worries about our Hamburg-administered assets were not entirely unfounded. When the Guardianship Office demanded from the assistant Dr. K. that he provide the commercial papers he had received, he was not able to produce them right away; in other words, the assets entrusted to him were not all in hand. Consequently, it took a long time before he was able to replace the missing documents. I cannot describe how I suffered during this time. No matter what the Guardianship Office reported to me or wanted to determine, I simply said yes, since I was unable to have any opinions or take any decisions back then. Putting all my trust in the God of my fathers, who alone knew my true internal state of being, I gave everything over to his care, all that, in my ignorance of these new conditions, I was unable to even remotely understand.

---

70 Administered as chloral hydrate, this pharmaceutical sedative was widely used to counter insomnia, starting in the latter part of the nineteenth century. It was first formulated and promoted in Germany and found a ready market as an inexpensive, easy-to-use drug, despite its addictive properties and overdose risks (with no effective reversal agent), in addition to potential for abuse (also known today as knockout drops and the date rape drug). See, for example, E. Shorter, *Before Prozac: The Troubled History of Mood Disorders in Psychiatry* (2008).

/One day I was called to the Guardianship Office. They informed me that the commercial papers that had been received from Hamburg included the obligations of the Hungarian Northeastern Railway, which, in light of their uncertain value, could not be accepted as guardianship funds, but would instead need to be sold. I was, however, further informed that the value of this particular railway was no longer anywhere near the price at which they had been bought and that this sale was expected to result in a significant loss. With this news, I decided to take these papers as my widow's portion, so as to spare my children from this unavoidable loss.

/Only now, after years of begging and pleading, was I finally able to have an overview of the annual income I could expect to receive. Even if the amount was only modest in comparison to the needs of daily life, I was still relieved to have a clear picture of my situation. My inherited portion, consisting of the Hungarian papers and a small fraction of the other papers, was now paid out. The agents, as explained, were there only to manage the underage guardianship funds, and may the widow take care of herself. All German widows were covered by this merciless, one-size-fits-all statute, whether they were born near the Elbe or next to the Indian Ocean. Who cared if I, coming from a foreign land, did not immediately grasp and understand the intricate conditions? No one but myself.

/I was most kindly advised to bring my commercial papers to a bank for safekeeping. This I did. After some time, I took the usual trip to the bank in question to withdraw the interest accrued. But instead of the money I expected came rather shocking news. I was given the following terse message: The stock of the Hungarian Northeastern Railway had gone down significantly in value in the past days, and bankruptcy was feared. Do you actually understand what these few words meant for me? Effectively, if the railway company did in fact become bankrupt, I would go down with it, or rather because of it, and I would lose virtually my whole fortune. The bank advised me to sell the papers as quickly as possible. I was not ready to make that decision on the spot and promised to return the next day. With a heavy heart, I went back home. Instead of sleep that night, I had plenty of time to reflect on the actual value of my current assets.

/I was unable to come to any conclusion other than the position advised by the bank, since I understood absolutely nothing about these things. The next morning I was again advised to sell the papers, which then resulted in a loss of more than thirty percent. Just be happy that you are a fortunate owner of a plantation and have nothing to do with all these government and industry investments. Your plantation ownership is more secure than when you are compelled to invest your wealth in papers, whose creditworthiness is often cloaked in an impenetrable fog. You will not have a sufficient basis for comprehending these things, and how could it be otherwise! I was not much better off, despite having already spent a number of years living in the midst of such progress. And you will likely comprehend even less when I tell you that investing wealth in papers is incredibly risky. It depends on such an array of circumstances, like for example, crop failures, the frequent encounters of the various monarchs, the persistently recurring speeches of politicians, and many other serendipitous events. They can all cause the value of these papers to rise or fall, meaning one must always anticipate random chance.

/Although now safe from the arbitrariness of an assistant, I was entering a troubling period that required my precise calculation if I did not wish to fall victim to prevailing circumstances. My children's assets had been converted by the Guardianship Office to government securities, which are known not to produce much interest. When the amount owned is insignificant, the greatest frugality is required, if liabilities are not to exceed assets at the end of each calendar year. All my efforts went into applying this theory, but I often had to struggle mightily with the execution. You must not think, however, that I lived a life of unnecessary luxury and excess, not at all, but rather had a lifestyle that is considered middle class here. Despite all my computations and considerations, I could not do much to improve my situation. And meanwhile, the time was drawing closer when my children, according to the law of the land, needed to be sent off to school, in part because I was in no position to have them taught at home, as I would have loved to do. The private schools in Dresden are quite expensive, and with my limited resources, there was no chance of having my three children go to such schools. And so, I had no choice but to come up with means and ways—without an adequate grasp of their ramifications—to find a solution.

As happens frequently in life, I found myself in a situation where I resolutely closed my ears to reason and made room for my heart to rule. My mind frequently gravitated to the thought that told me it was pure obsession for me to keep holding onto my plan to give my children a German education. And yet, is the point not only and exclusively a matter of love toward the deceased? So spoke my heart. Whereupon my mind returned fire by repeating a hundred times that my poor husband, in his great love for me, never would have allowed me to lead a life under circumstances that required me to mobilize all my moral and physical strength to fight each step of the way. And my mind admonished me further: Now the time has come when you can move to a southern location with a clear conscience, where you have neither a harsh winter with all its demands, nor a duty to attend school. You cannot stay in Dresden over the long run, you can see that yourself, and what will you do then? Keep on trying, I thought to myself, as long as I still can.

Zittau or Weimar were suggested to me as places where the cost of living was lower. But I did not know anyone in either city, so I found it hard to come to a decision. Then someone suggested Rudolstadt, where I knew a Swiss woman and her family from my time in Hamburg. Through this family, I now gathered details about Rudolstadt, on rents, grocery prices, taxes, tuition, etc., all the things that make a difference when one does not have full pockets to transact costs.

/My first step was to discuss all this with my motherly friend, the old Baroness, who also encouraged me in this direction, even though it would be indescribably hard for both me and her. However, she feared I would feel isolated in little Rudolstadt, especially mentally. "My precious dear," she said to me, "the circumstances dictate that you need to move to a small town, where everything is cheaper than here in Dresden, but someone of your nature and manner will hardly feel comfortable in such a constrained environment over the long term. The views of small-town folk are very parochial, and even Germans who only know the big city rarely become enamored of small-town conditions." I told her I saw no other option and wanted to at least give it a try. "I do not need to tell you that I will miss you very much, but one should not be egoistic." Those were her words, and yet, I would be the one to miss her so much more because she was simply irreplaceable—and so remained.

Whereupon I terminated the rental, and let go the nanny, and tried to sell as much of the excess furniture as possible. From now on, I wanted to live in a smaller space and make do with only one girl to help with everything. Do you know what the phrase "girl for everything" means? Let me teach you! The girl for everything must cook (that is, if she can), get groceries, wash laundry, iron, clean, heat in the winter, open the door when the bell rings, and about a dozen more tasks. Hence, correctly, "girl for everything."

Steel engraving of Rudolstadt, mid-1800s.

/18

I traveled to Rudolstadt first and rented an apartment. Soon thereafter the furniture was packed and sent. Then I followed with my children and the servant girl. I had adjusted very well to Dresden and enjoyed life there, including my limited circle of acquaintances that was nonetheless far better than in Hamburg. The few families I had gotten to know over time were almost exclusively from Hanover or Prussia. I spent many a pleasant hour in their midst and received many signs of their love and friendship. I therefore bid very reluctant farewells to my loyal friends, but above all my unforgettable, motherly friend, the Baroness T. My heart practically broke as I said good-bye to her. She held onto me so tightly, until her son separated us, kindly but firmly, in consideration of her poor health. As he led her to her chamber, she waited a bit longer while I bid farewell to her children. Then she returned once more to draw me one last time to her noble, loyal heart!

/Did she perhaps sense that this would in fact be our last time on this earth together? Who knows? After this day, I never again looked into her wise and trusted eyes, never again heard the voice that had given me such courage and comfort so many countless times. Dejected and pursued by thoughts of our earthly condition, I returned home that evening to a sleepless night. It is good, and we can never thank the Highest enough, if we are allowed to stay of sound mind to the last, and yet, there are moments in life, when people would be decidedly happier if they, at least temporarily, did not need to think and feel so much. But the ways of the Lord are not ours, and no mortal has thus far been able to fathom exactly why fate decides when to favor us and when not. It is a problem that mankind pursues in vain.

The next day, I traveled with my children and the servant girl to Rudolstadt, with its most lovely location, and we put up in a simple hotel until our furniture arrived from Dresden. Later I happened to ask my acquaintance from Hamburg if there had been anything special going on in town the day we arrived, since there were unusually many people at the train station. With a hearty laugh, she let me know that it was all because of unsuspecting me. It is true that the landlord, from whom I had rented the place many weeks earlier, had not posed the question to which I was so accustomed: "Where are you from, my lady?", and had instead agreed to rent on the spot, presumably because he knew my friend's family well, the ones who had looked at the apartment with me. But after I had left, this worthy Thuringian apparently did not rest until he had figured out the nationality of his new renter. In any case, my arrival was duly featured in the Rudolstadt newspaper, which had piqued the town's curiosity.

Not that we looked very Oriental upon our arrival, with me wrapped in nothing less than a modern Scottish coat, and my children wearing their basic winter coats. This news was anything but pleasant for me, though, since I now had to fear that this would make my goal, to live as simply and withdrawn as possible, extremely difficult.

Initially, I had firmly intended not to make any social connections, nor even visit anyone. Was I not plenty busy simply raising and caring for my three children? I should say. But this intention was thwarted by the kindness of a friend from Dresden. This lady made it a point to introduce me to a local family. In addition, more than I wanted to know, I now also learned that all newcomers to town, in order for them to be considered part of respectable Rudolstadt society, had to visit all the local *Honorationen*. To be honest, I considered this last point somewhat childish, all the more because I put little stock in respectable society. But I acquiesced to the unavoidable and decided to seek out these honorable people.

/What, in fact, led me to take this step? That would be you, which is to say, my remembrance of you. I had to tell myself that people would not easily forgive a faux pas and could instead feel justified in accusing me—naturally from their vantage point—of a lack of good breeding. As it was, I had already come across the most wondrous ideas all over Germany about our lifestyle and upbringing, often to my utter astonishment. Apparently, we are viewed merely, to put it mildly, as primitive folk, devoid of any refinement. Aside from my own preference against having a large circle of acquaintances, which does little for the heart and instead promotes that much more unnecessary gossip about others, I did not want to give these dear people any unnecessary grounds to spend time deliberating the dearth of Arab decency at their coffee parties.

/I had the most important names of the relevant families given to me, with the intention of visiting them over the next few days. The list turned out to be quite long, but could not be much shortened, as I would have liked, because of all the family relations among the locals. I naturally started my excursion with the prince's family in the palace[71] and was able to conclude my visits after several days. You cannot imagine how boring these visits are, since conversations must always be so forced to keep up the appearances of mutual pleasantry. It felt bizarre to have to go from house to house to visit complete strangers with whom I had absolutely no connection. And everywhere I had to listen to

---

71 The stately baroque Heidecksburg in Rudolstadt, Thuringia, where Prince Georg Albert, born 1838, was regent at the time. Although he may have had some interest in the Princess from Oman and Zanzibar, nothing materialized. He died unexpectedly of pneumonia in 1890, unwed and without direct descendants.

the same conversations and answer the same questions. It was a clear stroke of luck for me to have seen the first light of the world on our beloved island—because I do not know what else these good people would have discussed with me. Everywhere I had to report faithfully on Zanzibar, the great fecundity of the land, the heat, and so on. Once, when a lady somewhat naïvely asked me about slavery and I gave her a factual answer, she was honest enough to acknowledge that our slaves were far better off than many of the poor Europeans, who must often struggle in anonymity to eke out an existence.

/The degree of cliquishness here struck me as greater than anywhere else I had been. This makes it very uncomfortable for the newly arrived stranger, especially someone who has social ambitions and is unhappy without a busy social life and large circle of acquaintances. I soon indicated to all that I intended to live a quiet and withdrawn life and therefore preferred not to attend any social gatherings. But that did me absolutely no good, as I still had to decline many invitations to avoid the frequent and fascinating afternoon gatherings.

Here I sent my children to school for the first time, in fact, all of them on the same day. I was quite unhappy on this day and constantly battled my gloomy thoughts. Oh, how much I would have wanted the children to be educated at home, if only the circumstances would have allowed it. Until then, I had looked after my children myself, day and night, even hour by hour, and watched over them like the apple of my eye. From now on, however, I needed to entrust them *nolens volens* to total strangers, if I did not want to get in trouble with the law of the land.

Wistfully, I embraced all three tightly the first morning they went to school, and it felt to me like they were about to embark on a trip around the world. They were all very animated that morning, full of anticipation of things and settings they had until now only heard about. On this day, the house felt deserted. I could not get comfortable anywhere and missed the incessantly bubbly bunch everywhere. From one of the windows, I could see quite far into the distance where the children had to return from school. And so I sat there, already half an hour before their arrival time, in order to spot them from afar. With quick strides, they rushed home, and when I met them at the front door, there was a rousing reunion. The previously still and barren house resounded anew with the voices of their lively company. The four hours of their absence struck me as endlessly long, and I thanked God when they were back around me. At that moment, I forgot all the bitter hours of my existence that were forever making my life so difficult. Today, their chatter never stopped. The names of the teachers and classmates swirled in my head for days, since it was impossible to talk to them about anything other than school and everything about it.

With this new chapter in the life of my children, a new period began for me as well. Accustomed to having the children around me, life between us had developed to the point that I often did not register their ages and instead discussed every happening in the house, all the practical things, yes, even our income and expenditures—as though they were adults. Their ability to quickly grasp what I shared with them always warmed my heart, and I was entirely fulfilled by them. Now that they had to be absent many hours a day, I often felt an oppressive loneliness that frequently also overwhelmed me with melancholy. In addition, I was not spared the less than encouraging feeling of how ill-equipped, in fact, an Arab mother is here, despite all her efforts, to be a mother of school-bound and fatherless children.

/In this country, it is apparently not enough for children to learn while at school, so they are also given a sizeable amount of homework, meaning they can never free themselves from learning. And then I was frequently expected to help my crying children do their work in subjects about which I, too, often had no clue. It also made me very sad to hear the children say—especially in the later years—that their classmates did better at their schoolwork because they always got help from home. I could not monitor the homework, nor was I in a position to bring someone on board for that purpose, so I often had to listen to the children's complaints without being able to do anything about them. As you can see, life is very complicated here, and an Arab woman does not come out unscathed if she chooses to follow her sense of piety.

/It was, however, only this feeling of piety that got me back on track the many times my spirit sunk, like a carriage seeking to stay upright in the thunder and storm, to keep its balance and remain firmly grounded. And yet, I was often so close to being overwhelmed, at any moment, and cast into ruins. Or did I have any attachment at the time to Western education? Heavens no, absolutely not, for I did not even know back then how to understand what all this education meant.[72] Perhaps I was not yet sufficiently Europeanized to be able to render homage to the prevailing approach here, that children are supposed to strive for better positions, better standing, etc. later in life than was bestowed upon their ancestors. Namely, this is the method that epitomizes the much beloved word "progress." Since we back home are still in baby shoes, so to speak, as far as fully appreciating this characterization, nothing was further from my mind than this specific intention. Our practice, which has existed across centuries until now, and by which the children, especially the sons, are proud to become what their parents and grandparents were before them, has no currency here, and such a viewpoint is considered long passé. The label "conservative" no longer has the meaning it once had.

My children had been in school only a few days when they stormed into the house terribly excited and overheated, surprising me with the totally unexpected question: "Mama, is it true that you are really a princess, please, please, tell us!" How should I have answered? I could only draw them into a deep embrace. Apparently affected by my reaction, they began to sob heartbreakingly, and even their midday meal did little to cheer them up. When I asked who had told them, S. responded that a classmate, an officer's son, had said it to him, and

---

72 The author uses the word *Bildung*, a word that means something more than education and can be said to include a socialized upbringing, refined acculturation, and broadly acquired knowledge of the arts, humanities, and sciences—a Western notion based on Western perspectives and principles.

he had then told his sisters on the way home. Their childish ways prevailed, as they acted rather strangely toward me that day, and I could see how they kept watching me. They were apparently thinking of fairy tale descriptions the nanny used to read to them. Soon, however, this strangeness dissipated, and I was once again nothing more in their eyes than their loving mother, and they were as always my beloved little children.

As you can imagine, on this day my thoughts were largely with you, as was usually the case when my soul was heavy. With their innocent question, the children had evoked many wistful memories that did little to ease my current task. I also feared their childish lack of understanding and would much rather have kept them unknowing until they were somewhat more mature. For a time, I was besieged by legions of questions to be answered, arising from their childish imaginations. Only now did the things I had brought with me from the homeland start to take on meaning, with constant calls of: "Come! Come! Mama is going to open the big wardrobe, and we can take a quick look at her Arab things."

/19

Winter arrived, and so did the many dangerous illnesses for children. In November, S. got such a dire case of acute diphtheria that it was a miracle he survived. The doctor who was treating him had completely given up on him one evening. Despairing, I stayed alone in the sick room with my son, who had already become stiff. My soul wrangled with the Lord to save my child, who barely continued to breathe. Perhaps an hour or so after the doctor had taken my last hope, a hefty stream of blood suddenly gushed from the mouth of my motionless child, and this release also brought rescue. The child opened his eyes and recognized me. I forgot the doctor's urgent warning to keep my face away from his, to avoid contagion, and kissed this child whom the Lord had restored to me in his grace.

/Getting someone to help with caretaking was out of the question. Our only servant girl had to stay isolated with the two small girls and was not allowed to come into the sick room. Outside assistance was absolutely unthinkable. There were no deaconesses in the area back then, and the residents were so petrified about catching the disease that when my two girls walked out on the street, women walking towards them would detour to the other side. You can best tell how tremendously arduous the care was by the fact that I stayed on my feet day and night for the first week and never changed out of my clothes. My feet became so swollen that I could no longer fit into my shoes and instead had to walk in stockings, despite the fierce cold in the sick room, whose windows had to stay open under the doctor's orders. Even though the oven fire in the next room over stayed on the whole time, I never managed to get the temperature above 5° Réamur.[73] Barely was S. starting to regain his health when I, too, apparently as a result of all the anxiety and excitement I had experienced, ended up spending six weeks in bed and then another three months taking quinine[74] to fight the weakness and chills. I do not know what is customary across Germany, but in our case the doctor who handled the diphtheria took a double payment because, as explicitly stated in the invoice, the disease was contagious.

Spring had just begun when the two girls simultaneously got scarlet fever. S. had to be isolated, while I was so preoccupied with their care that I was

---

[73] Under the Réaumur temperature scale with water freezing at 0 degrees and boiling at 80 degrees, this is the equivalent of 6.25°C and 43.25°F.

[74] According to Professor of History Andrew Goss in "A History of Quinine Drug Hype Since the 19th Century," quinine was discovered as an effective anti-malarial drug extracted from the bark of the cinchona tree, but was also experimentally and incorrectly promoted in the nineteenth century as a cure for a variety of other ailments.

unable to attend to him at all. I therefore had him lodge with a teacher. At that point in time, I had a very bad servant girl, who hardly wanted to work and just took it easy. No surprise, of course, that she needed to do more now because of the sick children, which suited her even less. Indeed, lo and behold the emancipation of European servant girls! One day, as I wanted to get supper for the children from the kitchen, I found neither soup, nor servant girl. Since the apartment was not very large, it did not take long to conclude that the servant girl had, without saying a word, up and left. As if this were not enough, I soon also discovered that she had locked the door shut and taken the key. Now just imagine my situation. Locked in with two children beset with scarlet fever, and no one at all there to help, truly this could have been conceived and enacted only by the greatest perfidy. The fear that something might happen to the sick children overnight, when I would have no way to get care, disconcerted me so much that I yelled out the window for help. Because the house had a front yard and lay somewhat distant from the isolated street, there was no hope of getting help right away. At long last, someone heard me, and it took about another two hours before the door could be opened.

/There is hardly any way for you to comprehend what my life was like in the period that followed. How can you understand when I tell you that I had to survive for six weeks on end with two sick children and absolutely no help. I had to take care of every bit of work in the house myself, since I found no new servant girl for fear of contagion. Our fatalism is often mocked here, but I honestly do not know if their degree of trepidation is not worthy of pity. Even the disloyal servant girl later cited her dread of contagion as her excuse. I was completely helpless and abandoned by everyone. Initially, I saw no one but the doctor, a different one from the one we had when S. was sick. This new one was so humane that he helped with errands outside the house and even later assisted with the children's baths. An old seamstress, who had said she would occasionally come for an hour or two to help out in the kitchen or run errands, one day explained quite downcast that she was sorry, she could no longer assist me if she did not want to lose her other clients. What do you think about this kind of humanity? Better to do as I have done and put no stock in such vaunted terms, absolutely none. I have found that people generally are charitable only when it suits them. Even the heathens are persuaded and stand by this lesson.

/I became, as I said, the sick nurse and servant girl for everything. The doorbell almost never rang to disrupt my work, since it is apparently not the custom here, as it is by us, to call on the sick around us. Perhaps the fault also lay with the great fear of contagion. During this period, I lived through days that I will not forget as long as I live! In order to meet S. on the street or buy what was missing in the household, I had to lock my sick children up in the house, oh horror. I cannot describe to you in words how that made me feel. Perhaps the closest I can come to conveying it is how disgusted I felt to be alive.

/The hardest task for me was and remained getting the fire to start in the stove and the oven. Often I was still unsuccessful even after half an hour of trying. I know you too well to fear that you would laugh at me if I admit that I frequently cried bitter tears of complete despair. One day, it was so frigid, oh so bitterly frigid. I was crouched down by the cold and depleted oven, trying and trying to light the fire, when I was suddenly completely startled by the doorbell. I found the baker's boy with his goods at the front door. Seeing him there, I jumped at the thought that I could perhaps ask this boy to get the oven going in the living room. No sooner said than done. And look, how quickly the fire sprang into being with his practiced hands.

/I now had to head out to the promenade twice a day to meet S. and comfort him because the poor boy was suffering so much from homesickness. Meanwhile, the two sick children simply had to stay locked up in the house. Oh, how I hurried home afterwards to confirm that my children were still alive or had not somehow, as my extremely frayed nerves led me to fear, died from a house fire. During the day, I almost forgot how to sit, except at mealtimes, and not until evening could I take a bedside seat by the sick children and read them stories from Hoffmann and Nieritz for their entertainment. That was my only hour of rest every day, for once the children were asleep, I went into the small sitting room to mend old sheets and clothes.

Given these circumstances, the prospect of continuing to live in Rudolstadt was greatly spoiled, even though it was so pleasantly situated, and I consequently felt very unhappy here. Life in a German city is not advisable for strangers from distant shores for the simple reason that they will feel isolated in their perceptions and perspectives. The impulsive Southerner, who is averse to all affectations, has no sense for the countless ceremonies and formalities that the people here subscribe to so minutely. By the same token, more straightforward, natural individuals are then often labeled as naïve. And meanwhile, the views of people here are often so narrow that their interests typically do not extend beyond a ten-mile circumference. No, especially the ladies amongst themselves take virtually no interest in larger topics, and instead all the more in—their neighbors.

/With these and similar conditions, I regrettably did not find the life I sought, such that I could live quietly and unnoticed within my means. As unbelievable as it may seem, the good people here really knew exactly when I had bought a new hat, how long I wore my clothes, when I had last gotten a new ribbon, who came to visit me, and even more: what we had cooked for dinner! You are constantly being observed, and it feels like living in a glasshouse. At first, I ignored it all, but over time I really had my fill with all the pettiness. One day I received a visit from a complete stranger, a traveler to Africa, who was sent to me by a well-known family in L.[75] He had just returned from Zanzibar and wanted to show me the latest photographs from there. Since this gentleman was very tan from the tropical sun and sported a very black beard, these characteristics were enough for the staid Germans to stamp him as one of my brothers. And within twenty-four hours, pretty much everyone had something to say about it.

I eventually came to understand that a small German town is not quite the place where a foreigner from overseas will feel comfortable. In a big city, individuals are less watched and controlled and can much more easily blend in. One day I received correspondence from the Head of Guardianship in Dresden, to which a response from me in German was no easy chore, given my minimal understanding of bureaucratic and legal terms. I was rather troubled and discouraged, pondering the best way to formulate a response that would avoid any possible misunderstanding. My eight-year-old youngest daughter found me in this state when she came home. Since the age of three, she had called me "my child," and so she ran over to me and said in her childish way: "Child, do you have a fate again?" Namely, the word fate for her represented troubles, since she could not yet express herself any better. When I explained to her my situation, what I was thinking and how hard it was for me to draft the letter for the Guardianship Office, she called out: "You poor child, can I not help you? Tell me what you want to answer, and I will make a draft for you that you can just copy." And that is how it went. I told her what I was intending to write, and she, this eight-year-old, crafted the sentences better and more clearly than I could have done at the time.[76]

For more than a year, I was caught up in a particular thought that caused me countless sleepless nights, until I was finally able to come to terms with myself. The source of my struggle was no less the idea that I might try to give lessons in my mother tongue—or rather in my case, more like my father tongue—so

---

75 It is not known what location the author is referring to here.
76 Rosa's support, which began so early, continued in the later editing support of her mother's *Memoiren* and other writings. See more about this mother-daughter relationship in the translator's essay "On Collaboration" on page 126 below.

as to meet the growing needs of my children over time. My thoughts would always rush to you, and as a result, I always wavered, again and again. Which then led me to start my wrangling anew, as it seemed to me the only way to stave off poverty from my beloved children. The powerful traditions of our upbringing are not easy to simply shake off. We are conditioned to stay true to them, even if this fidelity can very often become uncomfortable, as in what I was experiencing at the time. But the love for my children ultimately proved victorious, and gradually over time, the decision ripened within me.

/In this mental battle, I amply felt that even my dear German friends would have little deeper understanding for my deliberations, if only because people here have a completely different concept of working women than we do at home. The view here is that work is ennobling. Where such attitudes govern, my perspectives would certainly have come across as backwards and even bizarre in their eyes. But for someone who was not raised with this philosophy of life from youth onward, and who is then induced to accept its message through cold and rigid necessity, taking such a step is certainly no trifle. Orientals are often enough criticized for being lazy and indolent. When seen from an Occidental lens, that may be true, except that this too often overlooks how contented Southerners are in general, which definitely cannot be said of civilized Europeans. In addition, the Northern cold makes a necessity of a thousand things, of which those who live in the South simply have no concept. The natural consequence is that people take virtually no pleasure in undertaking arduous tasks.

/In any case, I found myself still too beholden to my upbringing to be enthralled by the thought of necessity-driven employment. Since the death of my husband, I often had to work hard, indeed, often more than a servant girl would have done. I doubt such a one would have repaired her torn shoes, except in rare cases, whereas I at times achieved a certain virtuosity therein by improving my children's shoes with the remnants of old and worn kid gloves. But that work could all be done in private, without anyone needing to bear witness. And I did the work knowing I was not trying to earn any money, just wanting to hold things together. This constituted, for me at least, a significant difference. As I said, it was only after a long internal struggle that I came up with a plan, since I saw no other way out.

20

One day, my children came home from school just as I was reading a letter from one of my loyal friends, who was responding to my news about the step I had determined to take. This true friend as always wrote very affectionately and encouraged me to hold onto this idea, as she felt my intention to give Arabic lessons in Berlin held much promise. She also acknowledged with sensitive empathy the soulful struggle I had gone through to make this decision, so that when the children entered, I was in a somewhat emotional state.

/"Mama, what has happened, did H.[77] perhaps write something sad, please tell us about it!" Those were their first words. And when I explained the situation to them and shared the contents of the letter, they all let loose a hefty stream of tears and showered me with their caresses. After hearing the reason for my dejection, they all asked in their childish way what they could do, so that I, in their words, "need not do any lessons."

/The feeling that we must care for our loved ones, above all to be able to protect and preserve them from all the rigors of the world and their consequences, often gives us a totally unimagined strength, which succeeds in overriding all obstacles. In this way, we see our tradition: Pride and all the similar words gradually disappear, like ice under the hot rays of the sun. Here in this country, people very much love to praise what children are on the outside—in my view, much too much—in being bright and well-behaved, etc., yes, often enough as non-pedagogically as possible in the presence of the children themselves. These attributes mostly left me cold. By contrast, I felt indescribably happy to have the love of my children, which, coupled with the feeling that I would fulfill my duties to them as much as my strength would allow, helped me over many a hurdle.

My choice of Berlin did not reflect my inner conviction for a successful venture, since there was little interest in Oriental languages to be found there at the time, in any case not nearly as much as, say, in London, Paris, and Vienna. Had I been able to decide to direct my feet toward one of these three worldly cities, I might have, most likely, succeeded in my endeavor. But thoughts of my dear husband precluded any other choice. Whether I did the right thing, though, by following this feeling, in light of my situation, struck me later as very doubtful.

---

77 Professor van Donzel suggests that this may refer to Hermann Ruete, who apparently handled some financial matters for the family. E. van Donzel, p. 496. According to the Ruete family tree shared with us by Ursula Luther, a direct descendant of the Ruete family, this would be Heinrich's younger brother, Andreas Hermann Ruete, who was born in 1850 to Heinrich's stepmother.

/In short, I took a few days that winter to travel to the German capital to find a place to rent, leaving my children behind in Rudolstadt, as hard as that was for me, in the sole care of our servant girl. The matter was, however, not as easy as I had thought, since looking for a modest apartment in Berlin is no small feat. The number of stairs I had to climb as a child was negligibly small compared to the many I had to mount during those few days of my search.[78] After I had gotten a newspaper, in which the available rentals were advertised, and studied them carefully, marking the ones that appeared suitable, I embarked on my still unforgettable expedition. Oh, it was so bitter cold, and the streets seemed paved with ice. At one point, before I knew it, I had slipped on the Leipzigerstrasse, directly in front of a little sentry box. But this disciple of Mars, standing at his post, just calmly watched me, as my repeated attempts to get up on my own proved unsuccessful. Finally, a humane civilian helped me get on my feet and order a coach. After minimally pulling myself together again, I continued my journey, up and down the stairs.

Not that I desired a rental on the second floor, oh no, I no longer dared to aim for this craving, after prices had thwarted that option. It is well-known that the second floor is only for the favored few. And since I was not part of that group, it was not hard for me to quickly comprehend the situation. I still very well recall how you described your pilgrimage to Mecca and the trials you suffered. It is of course to be expected that a trip in the desert would bring many discomforts, but I would counsel you to never undertake a journey like mine, to look for an apartment in Berlin as a complete stranger and completely alone in the very cold month of January. Finally, after much walking back and forth, I was able to rent a ground floor space with four small rooms, but, of course, situated so that the two back rooms had practically no view of the sky, much less the dear, enlivening sun, while the two front rooms looked onto an imposing wall of multi-story apartment buildings. And for a residence like this, people demand a rent that borders on disbelief.

As part of my move to Berlin, I let the Thuringian servant girl go and thus embarked on the trip with my children alone. Already on the train, the eldest began a heavy fever, and once in Berlin, came down with chickenpox. We stayed in a simple hotel the first few days, until the furniture arrived, and I was able to hire a servant girl. With the latter, it was not long before I made a very bad discovery, when she ended up so drunk one day that she had to be removed from the house with help from the police. On top of that, this episode even landed me in front of the court. Would you have thought something like this possible? I

---

78 The author's childhood home, Bet il Mtoni, was known for its extensive stairs (*Memoirs*, p. 5).

certainly least of all! For us, all of mankind stands equal before God but nowhere else, whereas here, this so-called enlightenment, which levels everything off, makes everyone equal. In short, I had to appear before the judge to testify against the woman because she had assaulted a policeman. I was quite surprised to find a long article in the morning paper a few days later about my humble self. Much was rehashed about me in this piece, and even my plain attire was described. How else would they fill the long-winded columns of the paper, without resorting to such trivialities. If only the correspondents and reporters could stick to the truth, then that would even be acceptable, but—but!

I was deeply touched to discover that the ladies of Berlin follow English and Arabic custom by initially welcoming strangers to their city. In this way, strangers soon feel at home, especially when they, as in my case, are fortunate to meet high-minded, selfless people. Oddly enough, Berlin is the only city in Germany where I felt somewhat at home, even though I appreciate the calm and peaceful life in the countryside more than the endless commotion of the big city.

Steel engraving of Berlin, mid-1800s.

/Now I began to think seriously about the purpose that had brought me here: giving lessons. According to the advice of my newly-won friends, I should "simply" advertise in the paper. The first advertisement I placed for Arabic lessons was anything but "simple" for me, as it felt to my disheartened soul like an epitaph for my own tombstone. Heavy-hearted, I was nevertheless very grateful to the gentlemen of the *Kreuzzeitung* and *Norddeutsche Allgemeine Zeitung*[79] for their generosity. The gentlemen would not accept any payment for the advertisements, and the latter even printed theirs in especially large letters. My first pupil reached me, however, not through the newspapers, but through the kind recommendation of one of my acquaintances, which was a great relief. This way I could rest assured that the pupil in question was a respectable person, whereas that cannot always be so clearly ascertained with an advertisement. Spare me any further description of the first lesson I ever gave in my life, as it was the first time I had to earn my keep by the sweat of my brow.

/Later other pupils followed. I often had to repeat a single word five to seven times until they were able to pronounce it more or less correctly. You cannot imagine how much difficulty Europeans have with the rich vocabulary of our language. It is not like any European language, and our guttural sounds just leave some in complete despair. In response to my advertisement, I was soon getting requests from America, England, Holland, and Austria to provide instruction through correspondence. What do you make of this idea? One can conclude only that the letter writers had had no previous encounter with the Arabic language, otherwise they could hardly have come up with this suggestion. Unfortunately, I so often had reason to feel that this teaching profession, to which I had resigned myself after so much inner effort, was not made easy for me. It was impossible for me to ascertain upfront whether I would be dealing with an avid student or a hollow dandy. But nothing did more to dampen my ardor for giving lessons than the unsavory behavior of a Jewish couple. As an Arab, I myself am Semitic, so one cannot refer to me as anti-Semitic in the European sense. That Arabs generally disdain Jews and consider them unclean is, of course, widely known.[80]

In the meantime, I had swapped my ground floor apartment with a similar one on the fourth floor. Here I became very ill and had to take great care of myself.

---

79 Founded as the *Neue Preussiche Zeitung*, the *Kreuzzeitung* became known as the "Cross Newspaper" because of its Germanic Iron Cross in the banner and lasted until 1939. The *Norddeutsche Allgemeine Zeitung* had its roots in the *Leipziger Allgemeine Zeitung* that was founded and run by Heinrich and then Eduard Brockhaus. It later became the *Deutsche Allgemeine Zeitung* and lasted until 1945. See Wikipedia for "Deutsche Allgemeine Zeitung."
80 It may be noted that the author's son Rudolph married into a Jewish family and spent much of his later life seeking to mediate between Jewish and Palestinian interests in the period leading up to the creation of Israel.

Letters to the Homeland

Upon returning from a short walk with my children one day, I found a letter in which I was being asked to provide Arabic lessons in the home of the sender. This lady belonged to one of Berlin's richest banker families, and her princely residence was situated on the upscale Alsenstrasse. She explained in her letter that she was ailing and therefore could not climb my three flights of stairs. I intended to decline the request, but when I told one of the ladies I knew, she advised me for material reasons not to simply reject the offer. She argued that I should think of my children. Oh my God, as if I would not have jumped through fire had that been necessary for my children! So I wavered in my decision, all the more because this friend offered to go to this lady for me and speak with her, before I went myself. I learned that this lady was preparing for a trip to Africa with her husband and therefore wanted to learn Arabic. The plan was for two hours a week. I decided to swallow even this pill, since the feeling that I should not miss any opportunity for my children was once again the driving impetus for my actions.

/Unfortunately, my acquaintance had not discussed the hourly rate, and so I asked her to write my pupil that I would charge 10 Marks. Although I normally charged 5 Marks in my home, the long way, for which I would occasionally need to take a coach, in addition to the extra travel time, would justify the extra amount. Now guess what answer I received! You are unlikely to get it right because your thoughts are no doubt influenced by "noblesse oblige." And yet, such people have no sense for this "noblesse oblige," but operate instead on the basis of their slogan, namely that friendship stops where finance starts. In this case, there was no friendship to bring to an end because it had never begun, but rather the urge to learn Arabic. The response I received from this Jewish lady consisted of payment for the lessons provided to date—and a thank you for the remainder!

There was, sadly, little demand for Arabic lessons, presumably because at that time Germans had, as yet, little interest in the Orient. Later, I also gave lessons in Swahili, a language that is much easier for Europeans to learn. Often, I had to give lecture-style sessions to my students about all sorts of things, like the local inhabitants, the animal and plant world, climate conditions, food, religion, and similar questions. The main topic, however, was usually the question of slavery. It typically provoked wide-eyed amazement on the part of these good people when I answered their question, whether I myself had had many slaves, with a completely natural yes. When I was once asked how many slaves I had owned altogether, and I answered that I did not know the precise number because we did not keep records of such things, although the number surely would have reached many hundreds, the amazement took no end.

/It is rather astonishing how little objectivity Europeans bring to their judgments about slavery. There is a tendency to sentimentalize, often to an unbelievable degree, in ways, it seems to me, that practically equate slavery with cannibalism. These views are often so shortsighted that one cannot help but be reminded of the Biblical story of the splinter and the beam.[81] As if our field and house slaves had to work even half as much as the so-called free people that are doing the mining and factory work in Europe. And one should not forget the general military draft that applies in all of Europe, except England, where there is certainly not much to be said about any special freedom. One is forced to conclude that slavery exists here as there: here whites, there blacks. So everywhere the same. Just that people try to outdo each other in their assimilation, habits, and not least in their imaginations. As far as the practice of caning slaves, it is possible to have differing viewpoints. But even reasonable Europeans do not dare to completely reject this approach. Humanitarianism is a noble trait, and yet, its application with respect to each individual, as every person can attest from their own experience, is not always easy. The highly cultivated infatuation with humanitarianism here in the North differs from the limited drawing power such cultish behavior has on more sober, practically-minded Orientals. And who knows, in light of the shocking brutalities that are so rampant here, enlightened Europe may in the end be forced to take up caning after all, despite all its humanitarian efforts!

---

[81] Matthew 7:3: "Why do you look at the splinter in your brother's eye, but don't notice the beam of wood in your own eye?"; Luke 6:42: "Or how can you say to your brother, 'Brother, let me take out the splinter that is in your eye,' when you yourself don't see the beam of wood in your eye? Hypocrite! First take the beam of wood out of your eye, and then you will see clearly to take out the splinter in your brother's eye." (Christian Standard Bible)

21

The increasing sickliness of S. caused him to miss a lot of school and fall far behind in his learning. You will surely want to know, what does the latter actually mean? The point is that everything in this country turns on the words "to learn." Whoever has learned a lot is, in the eyes of the people, already a made man—or a made woman. Woe, however, to anyone whom nature has not favored with such talent and who has learned little besides. This species of person—especially if he has the added misfortune of being allocated an empty sack—might as well be buried alive. Should he, however, wish to compensate for this inexcusable defect through his awe of God, his reverence for old age and sustained life, as well as his devotion to truth and honesty, he could easily become an object of the greatest pity. For such traits are no longer among the most desirable and are long since outdated. Everywhere there is talk of cases where one or the other person is to be pitied because they did not learn anything and therefore cannot become anything. For myself, as I said, I was completely unfit to be a mother of Germanic children, for various reasons. First, I was—according to German criteria—far from able to consider myself sufficiently educated, and accordingly also unable to fully appreciate the school's targeted results as the children's one-and-only task that would lead them to bliss. Second, I had no way to support my children in their schooling because I was unable to give them any help with their schoolwork, as German mothers are wont to do. As a result, the boy made only laborious progress in school.

Already back in Dresden, well-meaning friends had recommended to me that the boy be sent to the cadet corps,[82] not least because they believed this would be a great relief regarding the costs of education. But I could find no pleasure in this thought. As far as costs, I would have preferred to eke out a living with my children, even if that meant eating dry bread together, rather than carrying on a light and breezy lifestyle without them. Oh no, what would be the point of an easy life on my own when they were my whole being! And as for what ultimately mattered for their upbringing, I trusted myself to work that out as well, as long as God gave them a good, God-fearing nature. Were we not also raised by our mothers and teachers, and do we not ultimately owe it to their principles and perspectives that we have become who we are? Humility,

---

82 The *Königlich Preussische Kadettenkorps* was the German military academy for young boys from 1859 to 1892. Bensberg was one of the *Voranstalten*, or preparatory schools, where cadets received seven or more years of education before being routed into the regiments. John F. Morris, "Crucibles of Virtue and Vice: The Acculturation of Transatlantic Army Officers, 1815–1945," pp. 120–21 (Columbia Academic Commons, 2020).

tact, interactions with others, and setting a moral example, in other words everything the inner person needs, can be influenced more, in my opinion, by the parents' home than in a large institution that does less justice to each child's disposition. Then, too, such institutions present many, and often very bad, examples that are easily taken as role models by children who are not self-sufficient or fully developed, which in many cases wreck the later adult. Often enough I spoke with officers who strongly counseled against an upbringing in the cadet corps. Putting a child in such a massive establishment, which many of my good friends were encouraging me for the above cited reasons to do, ran completely counter to my nature as well.

/Oh, it was very bitter, so very bitter for me, to have to swallow this cold pill of civilization after all. Or should I now stop the journey, still only midway, and throw in the towel before the laborious work was done? Yes, had it been on my account only, I would have taken that step long ago, but the reasons you know so well called on me even now to persevere. Countless sleepless nights, which severely afflicted my already frayed nerves, dragged me so far down both physically and mentally that I finally rallied my courage and took the first step. Namely, I wrote to the noble and benevolent Emperor William I[83] and requested that my son be admitted to the cadet corps. As I wrote the letter, I comforted myself with the thought that I might well be declined, since I had asked for a full stipend, or, in the best case, be made to wait a year or more, while the child could still stay with me. I readied myself for this latter possibility by accordingly, shortly thereafter, extending my rental contract another year.

/This time, though, I miscalculated. A mere three weeks later brought the answer that the noble Emperor William I had arranged for S. to be taken up by the cadet corps. Privately, I had already been informed that the Emperor had immediately approved my request and that S. was to enter the cadet academy in Bensberg on October 1. Such a prompt resolution of my inquiry caught me completely off-guard, and the rapid enlistment did not fill me with joy, exactly the opposite. It was already September, meaning we would be separated very soon. This imminent enlistment also had a very dispiriting effect on the child, who had until then been very enamored of soldiers, the way practically all German lads are. He got quieter and quieter by the day and completely lost his robust appetite, although he was not sick. This circumstance made me even sadder, until I could not bear to watch it any longer.

/One day, I asked him if he would like us to move to Cologne, so that he could at least visit us every other week. Oh, how his face glowed when I said that.

---

83 Kaiser Wilhelm I, German emperor from 1871 to 1888, the first to lead a united Germany.

He was full of joy, and called out repeatedly: "Please, please, do come to the Rhine!"[84] What should I do now? Follow the heart or the head? I was cleft in two, since it was obvious that moving to the Rhine right now, just after I had extended the rental contract for another year and was still picking up new pupils for lessons now and again, would be unreasonable. But the shift in the boy's disposition, on the one hand, with the certainty that he would soon leave home, and his indescribable happiness, on the other hand, that I could perhaps be nearby, haunted me day and night and left me no peace. I could not even think of a potential move, unless the landlord allowed me to sublet the apartment at my own risk, but I resolved to at least give a try.

/The landlord, who was a very kind and accommodating man—not a common occurrence in Berlin—obliged my request, for which I was very grateful. I put an advertisement in the paper, and among those who came to assess the place was a lady who appeared to suffer from some haughtiness. After having given the rooms for rental a close examination, she also wanted to examine me. Specifically, she noted that I was having to get rid of the apartment as quickly as possible, even below value. When she asked why, I told her I was hoping to leave Berlin in two weeks' time, to live at the Rhine near my son, who would be joining the cadet corps on October 1. "So, your son will be joining the cadet corps in October?," she asked in astonishment, "how is that possible, when did you apply?" I told her that it had happened just a few weeks prior. Oh my! That really got her riled: "Is your husband perhaps a senior officer?" When I responded no, she informed me that she was an officer's widow and had been waiting for one and a half years for her son to be placed in the cadet corps. And she was even more amazed, considering that admissions usually happen only in the spring.

Happily, I managed to sublet the apartment at cost. Having been notified that S. would be transferred to Potsdam as soon as a spot there became available, I thought it best to leave the furniture in Berlin and settle with the two girls in a simple furnished room in Cologne. Through the great kindness of a family we knew as friends, I left the furniture with them for free, which gave me some significant relief.

During this time, I was plagued by persistent rheumatism that I had picked up in a humid summer house. Ever since the death of my husband, I additionally suffered from a nervousness that endlessly threatened to undermine what little will to live I still possessed, and what I tried to maintain for the well-being of my children. The

---

84 The Kadettenanstalt Bensberg was housed in Schloss Bensberg, now in a suburb of Bergisch Gladbach, which lies just east of Cologne and the Rhine River.

upcoming change in our humble existence, which was forced by conditions that positioned my son in a career that was so contrary to my preference, impacted my health so negatively that it took the most strenuous effort for me to take care of even the most basic needs. The list of things to be done to dissolve the household was endless, and with only a single servant girl left, I had to handle more than my health could sustain. Even past midnight, I would sit and mend the already defective curtains and the many clothes of the children, to the point where my painful, rheumatic hands and fingers often became stiff.—

/To top it all off, this was exactly the time I lost my beloved, motherly friend in Dresden. How deeply this loss affected me, I have no way of expressing to you. My heart was pulled in the strongest way to Dresden, to accompany my most unforgettable friend to her last resting spot. But with our departure so imminent, I was deeply saddened to accept the inevitable and forgo the mere twenty-four hours needed for a trip to Dresden. With her, I lost much, so very much that was—irreplaceable! Where could I now find the great love and understanding with which this rare woman had blessed me for ten years, as she helped me lighten my load? Who else would now understand me so fully, as she did from the very first moment we met? Or stand by me, with the love and comfort of a second mother, through all the hard struggles and conflicts? Surely no one, and so her passing left me feeling immensely lonely.

/Undeservedly, and thanks only to the great mercy of the Lord, I never lacked for good friends. And yet, among them all, no one could have taken her place in my heart. Many years have passed since her death, and still to this day, I have this special feeling whenever something joyful happens. I always recall her words that she made sure to say to me so often: "Up there, darling, I will pray for you and plead for you."

Thus I remained beset with sadness for the loss of my motherly friend as I traveled at the end of September from Berlin to Cologne with my three children in a third-class railcar. Through one lady's kind recommendation, we found a temporary stay for a small sum with an officer's widow in Deutz, instead of having to go straight to a hotel. The first of October, the date on which I was to deliver S. to the Bensberger cadet corps, came much too quickly for us all. Early that morning, I rode there with him on the train, leaving both girls behind with the landlady in Deutz. The short trip progressed in silence, for each of us knew only too well how meaningful these next hours would be for us. We still had a considerable stretch to the institute on foot before we could reach our destination. With every step we took, my heart beat almost to bursting from an indescribable inner excitation. It would not have taken much for me to simply turn around with my child and go back.

/We finally reached a gate and had to wait a while, until an officer called by a soldier came to us. He was a friendly, amiable man and also offered to show me around. We followed him everywhere, me in my distracted thoughts, only barely able to follow his descriptions. On another occasion, I might have listened with more interest to all that he was so kindly showing and telling us. Today, however, nothing would have been more welcome than to have the whole academy hurled to the South Pole, out of reach for me and my child.

/Now I was told that I should go to the nearby guest house and wait for the results of the examination, which S. had to undergo before the cadets would take him in. After a while, he came to the guest house to let me know that—thank God!—he had been deemed healthy and was expected to join the line-up at a set time the very same day. Quietly and without much delight, we had our simple meal together in the hotel before returning to the academy. Once there, I handed the boy to the relevant company chief, in whose division he was to stay.

The farewell was excruciatingly difficult for both of us. Even to this day, I cannot forget the last look S. gave me. In it, I could read so much pain that he was trying not to show. My child seemed to me like a sacrifice on the altar of loyalty—to my deceased husband, his father—that I had placed there.

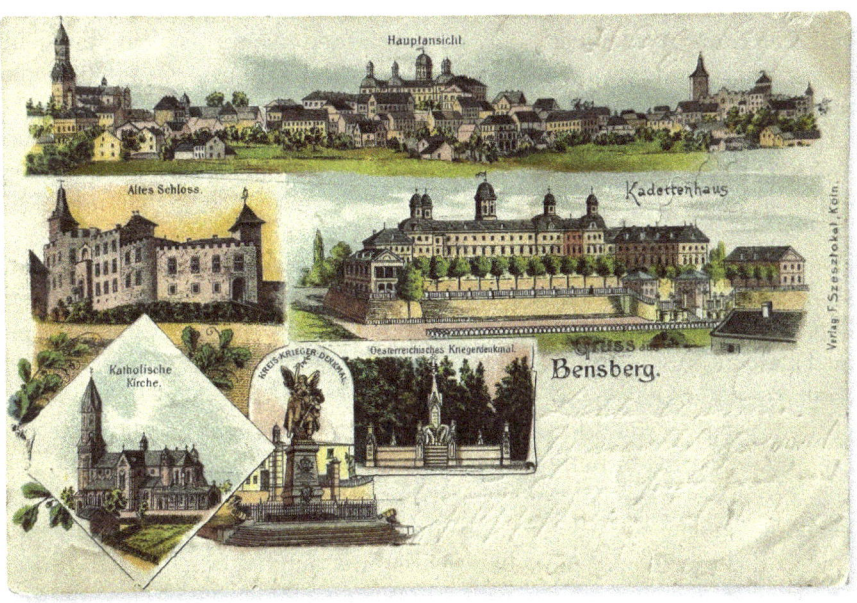

Colored postcard lithograph of Bensberg, late 1800s.

/Oh, how often had I wished to distance myself from the complicated European approach to life, where the individuality of each person only rarely finds room for its freedom of expression. Everything goes by templates here, and the individual numbers nothing more than one among millions. Out of a hundred residents, 95% are go-getters, and woe to any that take a different course, since they will simply be drowned. Everyone has to learn a certain amount to be considered capable overall, regardless of whether it is something they like or can do. Everyone is subordinated to the law and sharply monitored. Every nation here is like a big institution, and its citizens are just the wards, naturally without them realizing it. And meanwhile, the word "freedom" is in the mouth of every child. All those who do not want to stay a newspaper carrier, street sweeper, or quarry worker for their entire lives must properly equip themselves to count for something. There is no statutory or social exception for the children of an Arab mother. They must step up to the same level as the other children of true Germanic parents and traditions.

Feeling utterly dejected, I returned to Deutz to my two girls. It was now time to seek out an apartment in Cologne and let both girls go to school. As a widow of a German and living in Germany, the law obligates me to send my children to school up to a certain age. A popular girls high school that was led by an evangelical minister was recommended to me. So I went there and registered my girls for the winter semester. After extensive searching, with much back and forth on the rough cobblestone streets of Cologne, I finally succeeded in finding an inn in the old part of town, under the condition, however, that we did not have to eat in the restaurant area, but could sit in our own rooms.

/We were given two very small rooms with a view onto a narrow courtyard, so-called back rooms, to which the blessings of the sun had apparently been denied. As a result, the rooms were sullen, even on sunny days. It was one of the many gloomy days when we moved in, and I was overcome with the feeling—I do not know how—as if I had stepped into a grave that was above ground, where I would have to stay for the time being. I had no taste for the hotel rooms with better furnishings, that lay on the somewhat sunnier side, because for me they were simply—sour grapes! On the other hand, the landlord and landlady were both so good and kind, and tried to ease my way as much as they could. After two weeks, on a Sunday, S. came to Cologne on his leave to spend the day with us. Of course, he arrived in his uniform, which seemed much too large for him. My heart was truly in pain, as I saw him there in his altered attire, and since then, I can no longer stand the look of any soldier's uniform.[85]

The days I spent in Cologne in the two sun-starved rooms were often very bleak. I always counted the hours until my girls came home from school, since the two narrow rooms felt so cramped, oh so very cramped, to the point of suffocation. Only in their presence could I forget some of my misery. Every morning when they went to school, I was overcome with a wave of indescribable loneliness and isolation, often making me feel like I was in a prison. Under these conditions, it was also inevitable that my health would increasingly deteriorate, although my nerves suffered the most. The doctor I sought out for advice urgently recommended a change of air. That was easy to say, but where was I to go in the cold winter, especially when the children had to be in school? What could not be handled by quinine and bromide,[86] of which I had to take unbelievably large quantities, would simply have to go unaddressed.

At some point during the winter, we were invited to Bensberg for an evening presentation by the cadets. I went with the girls, and we were happy to see S. again, since he was allowed to visit us only a few hours every two weeks. On this evening, though, I felt especially sorry for the boy. I did not see much of him during the opening presentation, which he was required to participate in, but later noticed how quiet and listless he was about everything. I could tell that he suffered greatly from homesickness and still had not gotten used to life in the corps. But there was nothing to be done at that moment, despite my deepest regret. It was simply something to get through.

If there was anything to console me while here in Cologne in my dank back rooms, then it was the warm attention of a couple I had the joy of getting to know through a recommendation. As had already so often been my fate, in a life that was anything but roses strewn on my path, here, too, I found good and noble souls that sought to ease my way as best they could. I owe this family much gratitude for so much good, including the comfortable hours that I spent in their house, which distracted me from my own pondering and brooding. Alas, there is nothing harder than being far, far away from your own when having to endure the blows of fate that come from on high and sometimes also from the hands of men. It is only in foreign lands that one discovers what one has lost in the homeland.

---

85 Likely around the time this was being written, probably around the turn of the century, the author's daughter Rosa became engaged to Captain Martin Gottlob Reinhold Troemer, who as her husband continued his military career to become a Major and then Major General.

86 See footnote 74 above on quinine. Bromide was also a popular sedative in the nineteenth century, until its use as a calming agent was discontinued because of its long-term toxic effects.

/Because I felt so extremely unhappy, and because I could only write what I thought and felt, my letter correspondence became harder and harder, which led to steady complaints from my friends and acquaintances. I therefore burrowed into myself and often let months go by before I could get myself to respond to even one letter. A prisoner could not have yearned for freedom more than I did here, although I was completely free like all others to move around as I wished. My thoughts became darker and darker, and life seemed to become less and less bearable by the day. Death alone could have freed me from my agony, and yet I never feared it more than when I thought of my small children, who would have ended up with strangers. And this fear, fed by my bad health, often persisted for days and nights. In this state, it seemed that winter would never end.

/When spring came, I followed my doctor's advice and went to the mountains near the Rhine. This stay in the countryside initially seemed to do me some good, but unfortunately, it did not take long before I felt myself getting weaker and weaker until I could no longer move. Oh, I will never forget what impression this condition made on my two little girls. The summoned doctor was no longer able to feel a pulse at my wrist, and only a weak one at my neck. I was told that I absolutely needed to go to an invigorating seaside resort to overcome this abnormal weakness. But these doctor's orders were very problematic for me because it meant a totally unanticipated and unwelcome expenditure. My greatest worry was that I had no hope of taking all three children on this prescribed seaside trip, since the boy, who had looked so very emaciated and wretched in the corps, was due home just then to join us for his summer vacation. Of all three children, he was in the greatest need of recuperation, so that, bearing a heavy heart, I decided to take only him and left the two girls as boarders with a family we knew.

For obvious reasons, because I wanted to live and move about normally, I always, as a rule, withheld my birth name when registering in hotels, so I could live in peace and be spared the often very irksome gaze of the public. But such times unfortunately did not last long, since a carelessly addressed letter already sufficed to make my situation uncomfortable. Normally, I asked my friends and acquaintances to leave my birth name off the address, so that I could move around undetected in the summer season, for at least a short while. Here, in this remote area near the Rhine, a letter addressed to my birth name proved a bit costly. We had been in the hotel already two to three weeks when a letter arrived with the afternoon post, whose address contained the telltale word from my birth name. Because the innkeeper always delivered the mail to me personally, he would naturally have read the address. That same evening—shortly after supper—I was already made to feel the consequences. The innkeeper wrote me a very polite letter and quite simply informed me that he would from then on be kindly raising the hotel rate to such-and-such amount. This heavy-handed form of extortion was rather too blatant, especially considering that the hotel was still mostly empty, aside from the occasional Sunday visits, since the season was too early for the usual summer guests.

When the prescribed resort trip was over, I returned to Berlin, and S. returned to the cadet academy. Upon my arrival in the German capital, I was legally required to register myself anew with the regimented police. I did so, but who can describe my indignation when a policeman stood in front of my door one morning, wishing to speak to me personally. "Are you the princess from Zanzibar?" he began. Totally surprised, I responded positively, and he continued didactically, "You have three children, is that not correct? Two girls and a boy?" When I again responded positively to these additional, still inexplicable questions, he pressed further: "Well, why did you register only your two daughters and not your son with the police, and where is your son?" Imagine that!

/Now I could really see how far this lauded freedom actually goes. The police simply give themselves the right, without any solicitation, to meddle in family affairs. The fact that I bridled at such patronizing interference may well be due to my uncivilized nature, considering that, to my astonishment, the locals do not find this type of intervention to be anything of note. For us, such a question could at most be posed to a female slave, but never to a free person. From then on, I would not have been at all surprised if a policeman had come into our home from time to time to gather information about our food, clothes, activities, and social circles, to also exert some control over these things. I could not help but feel that I was in a strictly regulated institution, rather than a great nation state. Everything is so rigidly organized and maintained off a fixed template that even the very smallest deviation deserves punishment. Everything and anything is governed by statute, and the sections of the latter are as numerous as the grains of sand on the shore.

Our new apartment in Berlin was on Potsdamer Street, not far from the Botanical Garden. It had four tiny rooms, one of which had two windows, the others only one each. The doors were all tight and narrow, but the place was otherwise bright and cheery. We had sun in the mornings and afternoons, which was delightful for me. Life reverted to its usual routine. The two girls returned to their former school, and I took care of all the household matters, such as cooking, filling the lamps, dusting the furniture, and sewing and mending, with only the help of a so-called morning woman that often came in for a few hours before noon. If we wanted to take a walk in the afternoon after school, we locked the front door and took the key. When we got back home, I would always be ill at ease and check under the beds and sofas to make sure no uninvited guest had slipped into the empty apartment while we were away, which is not a rare event in a big city like Berlin.

/Quietly and withdrawn, I lived entirely for the children, as I never felt comfortable anywhere without them. We were always invited together because people knew I did not like to go out on my own. And to let them go out alone made me much too scared, since for me, the crosswalks in the lively streets were forever a source of enduring fear.[87]

---

[87] Consider the manner in which the author's husband died. See the translator's essay "On Fear" on pages 135–39 below.

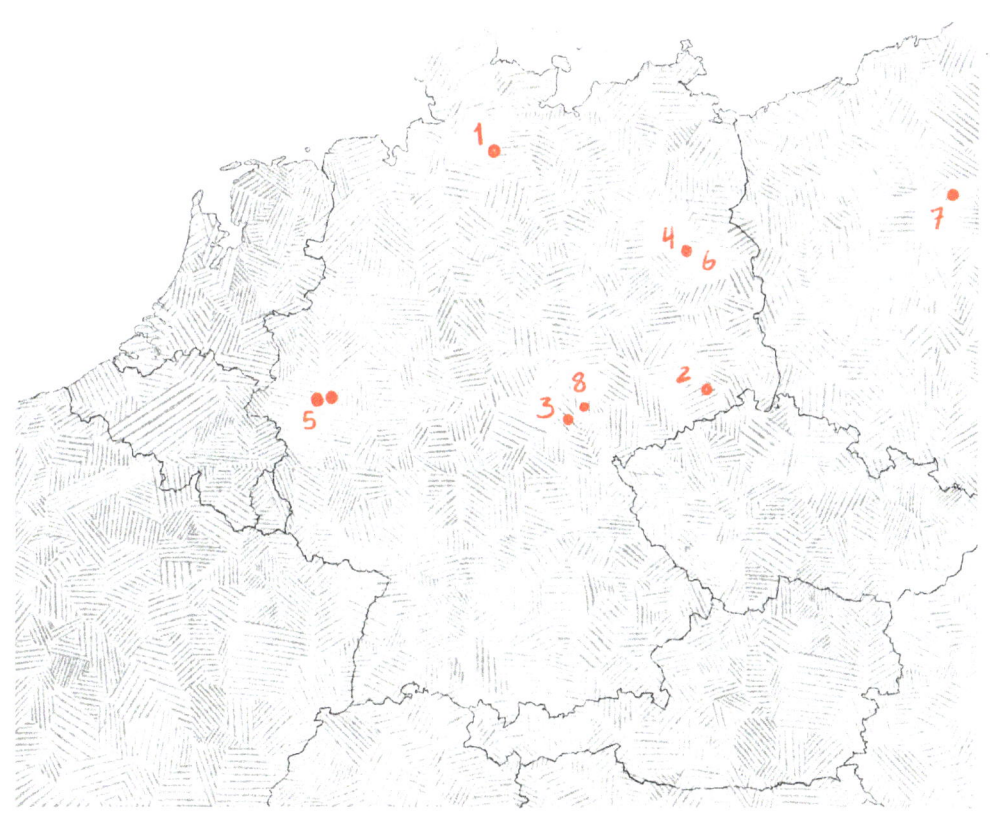

1. Hamburg 1867–1872
2. Dresden 1873–1877
3. Rudolstadt 1877–1879
4. Berlin 1879–1881
5. Cologne/Bensberg 1881–1882
6. Berlin 1882–1888
7. Bromberg (Bydgoszcz) 1914–1920
8. Jena 1920–1924

Map of places in Germany where the author lived (showing current borders).

The author with daughter Antonie and her husband with son Said in 1870.

The author around 1871 alone with her three children, Said, Rosa, and Antonie.

The author in fall 1884 with Rosa, Said, and Antonie.

The author sometime after 1885 with Antonie, Said, and Rosa.

ON COLLABORATION

Sayyida Salme was never schooled to write, and yet, she published a two-volume book totaling 400 pages of beautiful, animated prose in a language, alphabet, and script she did not learn until her mid-twenties. How was that possible? Some reviewers at the time speculated that the *Memoiren* had been ghostwritten, doubting the author could have come up with such an elegant and extensive account by herself. But we can now see from the historical record, from her handwritten edits of the *Memoiren* and especially from the hundreds of handwritten pages of the *Letters*, that this is very much hers. These documents are proof positive of her original authorship. They not only showcase her language ability after two decades in Germany, but also reveal the insightful and artful writing style as her own.

As a descendant of Rosa, her youngest daughter, I also take delight in knowing that Sayyida Salme had support within the family. Not to take anything away from the author's creation and imprimatur, we can see that Rosa and her mother worked together. It is lovely to recognize Rosa's even script alongside her mother's energetic strokes, as witness to this mother-daughter collaboration. Although we do not have early drafts of the *Memoiren*, the subsequent hand-marked edited version[88] and especially the two drafts of the *Nachtrag*[89] show the family interaction. The *Letters*, on the other hand, are different. With the posthumous discovery of the original manuscript, there was no opportunity for direct collaboration, but the children nonetheless made sure a typewritten, grammatically upgraded version would be available to us today.[90]

Studying this record has been both inspiring and validating for me. How special that I have been able to undertake this project with my own mother! In our shared endeavor of publishing first the *Memoirs*, and now the *Letters*, our roles are reversed. The writing is mine, but I have greatly benefited from

---

88 Leiden University Libraries Digital Collection at NINO SR 613 a-b. For reasons I explain, these edits were brought into my newly translated version of the *Memoirs*. See my essay "On Translating," *Memoirs*, p. 254.
89 The *Nachtrag zu meinen Memoiren* manuscript exists in three versions in the Leiden University Libraries: first, Sayyida Salme's original handwritten draft (Or. 27.135 A1); second, Rosa's original handwritten rewrite (Or. 27.135 A2); and third, a final typewritten version appearing right behind *Briefe nach der Heimat* (Or. 6281). The *Nachtrag* (meaning addendum) was intended to supplement the already-published *Memoiren*, presumably as an add-on for a re-publication that, however, never occurred. An English version is available in E. van Donzel, pp. 511–22.
90 As noted, Leiden University Libraries Or. 6281.

On Collaboration

my mother's fastidious and tireless review of my translations, comparing every word and phrase to the original German over many drafts, along with her ability to decipher the old German script, while also sharing her highly nuanced comments regarding meaning, placement, tone—all contributing to what we have jointly sought to make a most authentic rendering of Sayyida Salme's voice. Here we are, repeating the intense ritual of mother-daughter literary bonding with just a generation in between. I could not be more grateful.

Others have contributed to this book as well. The staff at the Leiden University Libraries, especially the front desk of the Special Collections room, gave us great support on multiple visits. They were very exacting on the rules, as custodians of these irreplaceable archives, something we truly appreciate. Also in Leiden, Anita Keizers, subject librarian of the Ancient Near East and our friend at the Netherlands Institute for the Near East (NINO), has been particularly generous in sharing her interest, expertise, and enthusiasm over the years. Extended family has played a meaningful role as well, above all Antonie's branch through Alexander von Brand, as well as Sarah Maria (née Ruete) Rothenbücher's branch through Ursula Luther, both of whom have warmly supported the effort with their family collections and memories. I also appreciate the support provided by B.K. Atrostic, Lark Bergwin-Anderson, Eija Pehu, Kathleen Ridolfo, and Alexander von Brand with their pre-publication reviews of this book.

We know ourselves to be part of a larger, international community of individuals who have supported and respected the memory of Sayyida Salme over the years. I can take this opportunity to thank all those who have come to appreciate her extraordinary life. That includes, among many in a long list, the Sultan Qaboos Cultural Center in Washington, DC, particularly under the leadership of Kathleen Ridolfo; Said el-Gheithy with his groundbreaking "Behind the Veil" exhibit in London in 2001 and his Princess Salme Museum in Zanzibar today; the Arabia Felix team in München led by Georg Popp; the German-Omani Association led by Wolfgang Zimmerman; Godwin Kornes, whose research focuses on Antonie Brandeis; Hielke van der Wijk, the creator and collector behind the remarkable www.omanisilver.com; Nasser Alrashdi, in Beijing's Oman Embassy, who gave me a copy of his booklet of selected Sayyida Salme quotes; and Michael Bauer and his family, who are related to us through Rudolph Said-Ruete and reached out to us many years ago in their own ancestral quest.

Of great importance is the tremendous work done by Professor Emeri van Donzel, who spent much of his lifetime exploring and preserving Sayyida Salme's life and writings, culminating in his remarkably comprehensive book, *An Arabian Princess Between Two Worlds*. Also of immense value is the extensive work done by Ambassador Heinz Schneppen, reflected in his German publication of *Briefe nach der Heimat*, which has similarly enriched our understanding of the contours and context of Sayyida Salme's legacy. We can also be grateful for two other books that revived the story after a century and set the stage: Professor Annegret Nippa's seminal contribution in 1989 when she reached back and took the bold and consequential step of republishing the German *Memoiren* with her thoughtful commentary in *Leben im Sultanspalast*, along with G.S.P. Freeman-Grenville's well-researched and thoroughly annotated reissuance of the original English translation in 1981.

In addition to all this, I am very happy again to give great thanks to my steadfast book publishing team, which has seen me through every book I have written so far and somehow always manages to make time for me: for copyediting, Lauri Scherer, and for proofreading, Bob Anderson, of LSF Editorial, and for graphic design, Joe Bernier of Bernier Graphics. Ever responsive to everything I send them, they have been excellent companions on this splendid journey.

And finally, I embrace my dear son Max, to whom I, like Sayyida Salme, give my "thousand love." He has been witness to my efforts every step of the way, as my companion and cheerleader, my source of second opinions and illustrations. He is my ultimate inspiration to create for the next generation.

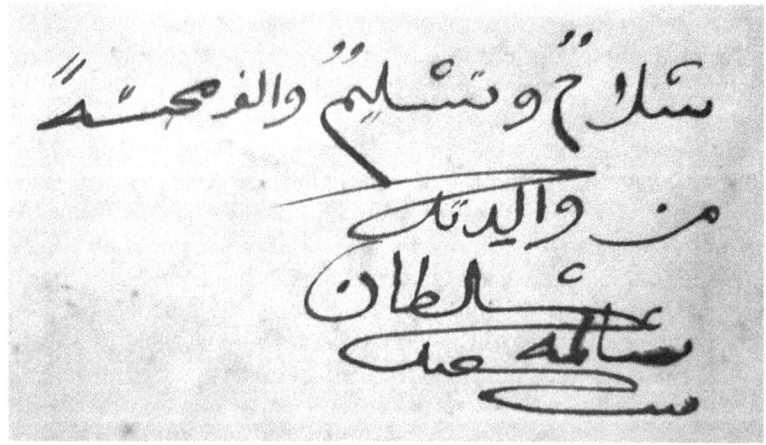

To her son: "Peace and a thousand love from your mother."

ON FREEDOM

It is tempting to read Sayyida Salme's story with a modern lens and see an arc of freedom. This Arabian princess, tied down by patriarchal culture and religious mores, unshackled herself by riding a Christian marriage into Western enlightenment and opportunity—or so this story goes. It is a narrative her *Memoirs* seem to set up, and there may be some truth to it.[91] There are, however, counternarratives that also ring true, and wrinkles that undercut such a facile, pro-Western view. With *Letters to the Homeland*, we get a different lens.

That the life of an Omani princess in Zanzibar was strictly regimented, severely limited, and heavily supervised is clear. Sayyida Salme lets us know, with some envy, that life at the top of the hierarchy was far more constrained for women than life at the bottom. Princesses could not show themselves to outside men without full covering, while common women were, by contrast, remarkably free.[92] The Sayyidas had all the privileges of being royal, but at a price, with almost complete sequestration from the male world and subjugation to the confining palace rules.

I have always thought it understandable that a free spirit like Sayyida Salme, who as a child enjoyed gun shooting and cock fighting (becoming "half an Amazon"), ran with the boys, and pranked with the best of them,[93] would find it difficult to simply become the demure wife of a designated husband relegated to a woman's world of bobbins and lace. Where to channel all that energy, intelligence, and self-confidence? Zanzibar seemed to afford her some latitude even after she became a young lady, especially out in the countryside where she could roam free(r) on her plantation and by the seashore, beyond the watchful eye of the harem and broader society. That is, until she was called back into the city, where her expansive spirit and society's tightening expectations were bound to collide.

Without a father or mother to channel their daughter into a straight and respectable lane, by encouraging a suitable husband and smoothing out the edges, Sayyida Salme had probably become a loose cog in a tightly wound

---

91 Some have even likened this story to recent attempts by other Arab princesses, like Sheikha Latifa bint Mohammed Al Maktoum, to escape their families, but those comparisons fall short. Sayyida Salme never sought to leave her family and was, in fact, devastated by having to lose her family.
92 "[S]ince such coverings are so unpleasant and disfiguring, high-ranking women avoid going out by day and frequently enough envy the Bedouin women who forsake such requirements. If such a Bedouin woman is asked whether she is embarrassed to go out without the required coverings, she will respond: 'Such rules are only for the rich, they were not created for poor women!'" *Memoirs*, pp. 108–09.
93 *Memoirs*, pp. 19, 30–31.

society. She normally should have been screwed back into place and married off before the age of twenty-two. It did not help that the family rift, and her landing on the wrong side of the divide, put a wrench into once functioning machinery. What a remarkably smooth ride the family, indeed the whole island and two countries, had had under their great patriarch, Sayyid Said bin Sultan.

Not that any of what became of our protagonist was inevitable.[94] Sayyida Salme made choices—she exercised her free will and took deliberate steps[95]— in opting to exit her clearly defined box and engage with a European man. That is, of course, the point. She allowed herself the luxury of self-expression beyond the point that society could bear.[96]

Part of a 1928 letter sent by the author's son to correct the record.[97]

---

94 Unless you put it all up to fate, a topic I consider in my "On Fate" essay in the *Memoirs*, pp. 239–42.
95 We can marvel at how deliberate her moves were once she decided to follow her love. In addition to sending many of her belongings to Germany on one of Heinrich's ships (E. van Donzel, p. 16), Sayyida Salme sold her property. I was stunned when Thomas "Dodie" McDow showed me one of his research finds: an official deed of sale from Sayyida Salme to her husband-to-be, in which she transferred her plantation estate, recorded by the clerk as "Kyajeenee," to Heinrich for $12,600 Maria Theresa thalers in late June 1866, not long after confirming her pregnancy and two months before leaving the island. Dodie's hard work in the Zanzibar and other archives resulted in his excellent book, *Buying Time: Debt and Mobility in the Western Indian Ocean* (2018).
96 That Zanzibari society could bear at least some transgressions seems enticingly clear from a quote Zanzibaris themselves told us came from David Livingstone: In Zanzibar "nothing is as it seems."
97 Quoting: "October 14th 1928, Sir Arthur Hardinge, Travellers' Club: My attention was called to your book A DIPLOMATIST in the EAST. On page 88 you mention my mother Emily Ruete. May I point out that she was not "carried off" by my father to Europe. She left Zanzibar on her own will on board H.M.S. "Highflyer" for Aden, was joined there several months later by my father, where they were married in the English Chapel, my mother being converted to Christian faith before...."

In theory, then, she ripped through the chains of misogyny and spread her wings, buoyed by love, for a life of free-to-be-me. But we are missing the punchline if we stop there and fail to read beyond the *Memoirs*. The *Letters* crucially continue the story. In this German sequel to her Zanzibar upbringing, scene after scene unspools a life in the West that proved anything but free. The German cultural norms were not only unfamiliar, but even anathema to her deep-seated values—and thus all the more constricting.

It is a tormented account. How to truly express herself when language—not just the words, but even the meanings behind them—proved such a barrier? How to freely interact when the weight of being the mascot and measure for all Arab society bore down on her shoulders? How to step up to her best self when she was constantly objectified, sexualized, mocked, and othered? This is often the immigrant's lament, but in her day and age it was especially acute, and in her case especially extreme, both in her face and behind her back. Sayyida Salme lets us know that the demands to fit in were oppressively incessant—and of course, she wanted to please her husband and fit in. But where she could not or would not adapt, especially after her buffer and protector was gone, she was either left out or sought refuge within. Both cases left her more and more withdrawn and alone. In some ways, apparently, the best way for her to fit in was to opt out.[98]

How tempting to imagine where her life might have gone had she been free to break into the Omani patriarchy. At the end of her first volume of the *Memoirs*, she tells the wonderful story of her great aunt who governed Oman at a crucial time, although Sayyida Moza never made it into the official narrative or family tree.[99] Thank goodness we have this written account! For her own part, Sayyida Salme came as close as she could when she served as scribe, financier, and co-plotter of the aborted coup. But even if the coup had succeeded, there is little chance that a promotion to a government posting would have followed.

---

98 This disconnect pursued Sayyida Salme as she moved from place to place in Germany, five towns in ten years, mostly driven by economics, but also social dynamics. Tellingly, after she finally dead-ended in Zanzibar in 1888, and no longer needed to shepherd her children in Germany, her next move was to a liminal space in the Middle East. There she stayed the next twenty years, a few years in Jaffa and the rest in Beirut, this cosmopolitan, mixed-culture, mixed-religion city—more of a "both/and" than "either/or" kind of place, where she could more readily be her composite, not conflicted, self.

99 *Memoirs*, p. 106. Sayyida Moza bint Ahmed was a daughter of the original Al Bu Said ruler, Ahmed bin Said, and her own daughter, Sayyida Azze bint Seif, became the first principal wife of the underage nephew she brought to power, Sayyid Said bin Sultan. Little is written about Sayyida Moza, but another good description appears in P.J. Ochs II, *Maverick Guide to Oman*, pp. 111–13 (2000). See also the family tree created by the author's son Rudolph, Leiden University Libraries Or. 27.135 E1, and the online Royal Ark compilation at Oman, Tab 3.

In this counternarrative of "freedom" gone foul, we might ask: What does it mean to be free? The hills and valleys of the United States, where I live, ring out with chants and rants of freedom. We are the "land of the free," and being free is a litmus test for being American. But the real test is recognizing that freedom does not operate in isolation. It is always embedded within society, and almost always a trade-off. Indeed, since time immemorial, one man's freedom has been another woman's yoke. Across the country, there is no counting the many ways freedom here creates or perpetuates limits—free to restrict abortions, free to ban books, free to deny medical care, free to impose religious practices. Even as America's exceptional freedom is exalted, restrictions rise.[100]

Now I am speaking *my* peace, so to speak—contributing my piece, the way Sayyida Salme was emboldened to do.[101] In this context, I would be remiss not to pick up the topic of slavery, where she took the freedom to express her views—her local concerns, drawn from direct experience—and for which she has been amply criticized. Even where this criticism is justified,[102] she also asserted what we can understand today: Freedom from bondage is only part of what we owe humanity.[103] Sayyida Salme called upon her audience—if it would listen—to consider the conditions of European factory workers, baggage carriers, stone cutters, and Siberian miners, or the fate of young conscripts being led off to war, all of whom were in bonded conditions, often much worse off than slaves living under Arab social tenets in Zanzibar.[104]

Taking a closer look, where did Sayyida Salme's leap into freedom leave her? This is where, I think, the *Letters* are the most instructive for us today.

---

100 Could the author have been more prescient? "It also seemed to me, over and over again, that most people, despite having written the word "freedom" on their flags, are hardly inclined to give others the same degree of freedom." (above at page 74)

101 "Having been born and bred in the East, I am in a position to set down the unvarnished reflection of my Oriental experiences—of its high life and its low life—to speak of many peculiarities, and lift the veil from things that are always hidden from profane eyes. This, I hope, will constitute the main value of my book, and my object will have been fully gained if I have been able to contribute my share, and above all, if I have succeeded in removing many misconceptions and distortions current about the East." *Memoirs*, Afterword, p. 229.

102 See my essay "On Controversy" in the *Memoirs*, pp. 243–51.

103 I am struck by Sayyida Salme's biting humor when she recounts what happened after the British-held slaves on Zanzibar were freed: "Meanwhile, the humane emissaries of the anti-slavery associations went silent. They had accomplished their goal and freed the poor victims from slavery, a status unworthy of any human being. What was now to become of these slaves was no longer their concern. Or at most, their ladies, to complete the nonsense, knit wool socks for the residents of the hot South." *Memoirs*, pp. 165–66.

104 On the wide variety of slave experiences in East Africa, see Thomas Vernet, "East Africa: Slave Migrations," in *The Encyclopedia of Global Human Migration*, ed. Immanuel Ness (2013). Said a Captain Mignan of Oman in 1825: "My residence in Arabia has convinced me that a slave may be perfectly happy; and I feel persuaded that his condition, when compared with most of the peasantry of Europe, is in every respect the more fortunate of the two." Excerpted in R. Said-Ruete, *Said bin Sultan (1791–1856)—Ruler of Oman and Zanzibar: His Place in the History of Arabia and East Africa*, p. 158 (1929).

Her choice of husband, her willingness to transgress, her resolve to keep going and not turn back—these became reinforcing layers in direct decisions she made over and over again, at her moments of greatest distress when the harsh reality bore down on her. The answer is, page after page if we can absorb it all: It left her in a deeper sinkhole than she could ever have imagined.[105]

Who knows, if her husband had survived and the two had thrived, if an unimaginable tragedy had not followed her unthinkable travesty, what counterfactual she might have had? Or if she had never even met her Heinrich? I will let someone else write the thesis of the many ways nineteenth-century women in the East had more agency, room, and opportunity than their peers in the West, a topic Sayyida Salme herself raised. Someone else may well consider the many ways Sayyida Salme escaped one set of limits only to land in another set of constraints that kept her from being free—in relation to society, her God, and herself.

The challenge is apparent. In the enlightened West, we like to think of freedom as quintessential to self-expression and success. But in Sayyida Salme's trajectory, especially when compared with her slave mother Djilfidan, we see that freedom is no free-for-all, no panacea. It takes at least some sense of security to be our best selves. The great flourishing of societies in history comes during periods of great stability. How else to understand the amazing Omani story under a Sultanate that has lasted longer than the American republic and yet is a monarchy, under much benevolent leadership over the generations, but not a freedom-loving democracy?

As I read our author's story, it took only one generation to transition from slavery to royalty, from *surie* Djilfidan to princess Salme, under the generous rules of progeny within Omani-Arab society. This leap from deep down on the totem pole up to the very top, from being a slave to owning slaves, hundreds if not a thousand slaves, pivoted on a single birth. But as we turn the page and move from the *Memoirs* to the *Letters*, it also becomes clear that it took less than a generation to go from the height of security and well-being to deep poverty and privation. Compared to her mother, social status went way up for Sayyida Salme, but then freedom intervened, and her social welfare went way down.

---

105 In her own words: "A prisoner could not have yearned for freedom more than I did here, although I was completely free like all others to move around as I wished. My thoughts became darker and darker, and life seemed to become less and less bearable by the day." (above at page 118)

We need not caricature this as an East-to-West fable. Clearly, a host of specific circumstances converged in the case of Sayyida Salme. But even so, it is hard not to see this descent from stable security to insecure freedom as emblematic of the closed cocoon of the harem (already a privileged place, even for the enslaved *sarari*) [106] vs. the brutal openness of the nineteenth-century Western industrialist, capitalist, consumerist revolution. There was not much of a German safety net back then,[107] and German society did not much know what to do with a far-flung princess, an Arab turned Christian, an exotic. It is perhaps just an isolated case, as opposed to a parable for her or our times, but still incredible to see how Sayyida Salme lost almost everything by exerting her freedom—everything but her dear children, a trace of royalty, and whatever she managed to salvage and build.

I suggested in my essay "On Fate" accompanying the *Memoirs* that fate is the foil of free will.[108] Here I will ask if freedom is the foil of security. The more choices Sayyida Salme took on, choosing even the unthinkable and unpardonable, the less stable and secure her position became—indeed, the more vulnerable she became to the vagaries of life, the machinations of detractors, the whims of custodians, the heft of government bureaucracies (a "pawn" on the colonial chessboard), and the insensitivities of the insensitive. Hers is an especially stark story, spanning the extremes from royal privilege to roiling poverty, but may still contain a kernel of recognition for all of us. Who has not seen that greater agency can bestow power, but standing alone can be disempowering? Maybe we are as strong as our connectedness. Maybe the allure of freedom is best tamed by the advantages of community.

Or maybe the lesson is also more direct. No one should have to self-exile to self-express. If someone seeks to act freely to be themselves, that need not imperil our own sense of self and security and provoke a negating response. We can strive to be more tolerant than that. Today, mostly we do, but only mostly.

---

106 Notably, the Arab harem afforded both protection and eventual freedom, in that Djilfidan became free upon Sayyid Said's death. But even then, she continued to benefit from the comfort of the harem and was amply provided for with the plantations and funds inherited by her royal daughter.

107 Germany did not even become a unified republic until 1871, after Sayyida Salme had arrived in Hamburg. Because her husband died in 1870, he was never a German citizen, only a citizen of the Free Hanseatic City of Hamburg. When Emily Ruete took the official step as a *Bürgerwitwe* (resident widow) in 1872, she was named a citizen of both the State of Hamburg and the German Reich.

108 *Memoirs*, p. 240. Simply put, what is ordained by fate is not a result of free will; what is decided by free will is not due to fate.

ON FEAR

After reading *Letters to the Homeland*, one might hypothesize that freedom is correlated to fear. The more Sayyida Salme loosed her moorings, the more vulnerable she became, the less secure, the more she had to fear. Perhaps this is too speculative of me, as I tread on the thin ice of conjecture. The clues I find are liable to crack under the weight of my presumptions, and I do not mean to distract from her own voice or descend into fictional musings. But I cannot resist saying a few empathetic words about fear, her fear.

I start with the last line of the *Letters*, which grips me, especially her last word: fear. And thus her long discourse ends abruptly—wasn't there more to recount as her struggles continued? But as I sit with her last thought, I find it circles back, and back again, and could not be more poignant.

When she finished, did she simply run out of time, ink, or interest? She does not put a stamp on it and say "I have concluded, here is a nice little bow to wrap it all up, now you have my story." No, there is no finishing touch, no rounded edge; the ink ends, her pen lifts, and she is done. This is the end of her long run, her uphill climb, her marathon. She gave us what she had, and then maybe, just maybe, a rush of emotions, a flood of memories wiped her pen clear off the page. I am done.

At first glance, she takes her leave with a quotidian thought—watch out at crosswalks—that she could have buried somewhere in her long account that has no chapters, paragraphs, or even indentations. But it was her last thought. And I think, if we connect the dots, she did leave us with something more meaningful:

> Quietly and withdrawn, I lived entirely for the *children*, as I never felt comfortable anywhere without them. We were always invited together because people knew I did not like to go out on my own. And to let them go out *alone* made me much too scared, since for me, the crosswalks in the *lively streets* were forever a source of *enduring* fear. (above at page 120, emphasis added)

Thus ends the story, and it is perhaps a bit odd that crosswalks would be so scary, even if she feared nothing more than harm to her children,[109] or was projecting her own fears onto them. But now let us consider her words—specifically, the four italicized keywords—more closely:

Keyword *alone*.

Sayyida Salme refers to her children, but she could just as well be referring to herself, as she says "on my own." For this is what she had become—quiet and withdrawn—a different form of sequestration than the one in which she had grown up. So many forces had compounded to make her alone; being alone was both a result of and remedy for a treacherous world. We might ask, for example, in all her dire scenarios, where were her in-laws? Where were her good friends? I do not have the answers, but perhaps it was some combination of her not knowing what to do with them, and them not knowing what to do with her. Sayyida Salme gives us cascades of examples where she was othered or ogled, as an object of fascination, even titillation—verily, a victim of the Oriental stereotypes she wrote her *Memoirs* to dispel. Others may have supported her up to a point, but she was probably socially shunned, at least by wives who did not need an attractive, exotic, single woman floating around. Even today, couples invite couples. It was hard enough when her husband was still alive, but how could she have felt at ease on her own without the social currency—language, culture, custom—of a Western upbringing? Exposing herself in public invited danger for herself and others. Keeping to herself afforded security for herself and her children.

Keyword *enduring*.

Unabated, exacerbated, this was her journey without respite. Some things cannot be undone, and consequences may take their endless toll. In her case, we see that self-expression beyond the bounds of social acceptance did not go unpunished, and exile was not for the faint of heart. Indeed, there is hardly a more moving passage than Sayyida Salme's anguished inner lament as she and her husband headed to the train in Marseille. It was just the beginning of her physical and metaphysical journey from East to West, Orient to Occident,

---

109 This greatest fear even kept her alive: "Death alone could have freed me from my agony, and yet I never feared it more than when I thought of my small children, who would have ended up with strangers. And this fear, fed by my bad health, often persisted for days and nights. In this state, it seemed the winter would never end." (above at page 118)

South to North, the first steps that led to all the rest. Fearful and conflicted, she nonetheless persisted and endured:

> As we drove from our hotel to the train station, I was gripped by such an unfamiliar fear that I would have preferred to scream out loud. I had the feeling as though, from this moment on, my homeland was being pulled ever further from me, and all the bridges were crashing in behind me. The cry of my soul for you turned into a thousand voices from my beloved island, all seemingly calling to me in unison: "Do not go any further, better to return again!" I fought a terrible fight within myself. Like an automaton, I stepped into the train that would now seek to take me, as quickly as possible, to an unknown land, to total strangers, as if I was in the greatest hurry to reach my future destination. And so we kept on riding toward the North. (above at page 6)

Keyword *lively streets.*

And here is the kicker. We could take her last lines as an unremarkable concern of a typical mother of young children, or we could look just below the surface and recall how the author lost her husband. This is not just any crosswalk, nor simply the bustling streets of a hustling city; this is a deep and searing memory, one that today would likely be diagnosed as PTSD. It is the trauma of seeing her husband lie there with a crushed body and delirious mind, the last wisp of life draining from him. He was her all. The year was 1870. She had hardly begun to settle—and the latest traffic innovation, the horse tram riding on rails, was new and exciting. Hamburg, as part of the vanguard, had inaugurated this form of transport only a few years earlier in 1867. Sprightly young men, including Heinrich at 31, had no reason to fear as they sprung lightly off the moving platform into the streets to reach their destinations ....

Keyword *children.*

Even in the *Memoirs*, Sayyida Salme tells us how devoted Arab mothers are to their children. She also had a good role model in her own mother, Djilfidan, who lost her first daughter early on and clearly loved Salme above all. This closeness was intensified, if possible, when Sayyida Salme had her own children. If there was one thing that never wavered, one thing that was her truth and purpose on earth, it was her responsibility to and love for her children. I, like many mothers, know what it feels like to be grounded and centered in this miracle of creation. And yet, my single motherhood has no comparison to the circumstances and complications that made Sayyida Salme devoted beyond measure. For her, it is like a current that circles around and around, that never lets loose, but surfaces over and over again in her discourse—her fear of not making it, of not being able to follow through—in this deliberate and defiant, even delusional, choice to raise her family in Germany in her husband's memory and honor. Does she define it, or does it define her? She is anchored to this precept even when the sea feels bottomless. As though she has no agency or identity left, but for her children, the only tie that still binds.

Such maximal attachment might be enough to instill an almost obsessive fear of loss, but there is more. Her husband was not the only loss that rocked her world. She also carried an earlier loss, a private loss, a devastation she apparently never spoke of, much less wrote about—that most unnatural loss of a parent losing a child. When she despaired about crashing bridges, she was mere hours from this calamity. Her first son, little Heinrich, born in December of the prior year, died en route, somewhere between Lyon and Paris. Retribution for sin, opprobrium for audacity, the wrath of God?—what all she might have felt. It was surely a defining moment in the life of a new wife and new mother, too painful, too taboo, too unspeakable. As far as we know, not even her children ever knew of this sibling they had lost. With the passing of her husband, the only one who knew the trauma of her sacrifice, even the shared memory was lost. Today we know the truth.[110] Once the reader becomes aware, the silence is deafening.

What we may fear the most is the loss of what we love the most, what defines us. To lose the core of one's being is to face an abyss, enough to turn on the Almighty, as Sayyida Salme admits to doing in her darkest moment (above at page 55). With her losses, she also had plenty to fear in a world that left little room for being different. As she says of life in the West, "[W]oe to any that take a different course, since they will simply be drowned" (above at page 116). But if we care to read deeper, her last sentence reveals her essence. Here is a proxy for her daily triage to overcome her traumas, to find and make her way on the crosswalks of those all too lively streets.

---

110 Heinz Schneppen, who served as German Ambassador to Tanzania from 1993 to 1996, retrieved a record of the infant Heinrich's death from the Hamburg *Staatsarchiv*, while doing research for his 1999 publication of the author's *Briefe nach der Heimat*. H. Schneppen, *Briefe*, p. 174.

On Fear

I choose to read her last sentence as an acknowledgment of fear that is in fact an affirmation of love. If we know the back story, it tells us that her losses—of her homeland, her family and friends, her firstborn, her husband—would not prevail. She would find her way, alone, on her own, with and for her children, determined to protect and persevere—as she did. She ends on a note of fear, but in a paragraph that starts with love. In all her writing, I hear her say that fear is no match for love. Not from the shores of Zanzibar, nor on the seas of life.

ON INSPIRATION

Why should writings by someone who came from circumstances beyond our imagining, who grew up in a distant thousand-and-one-nights setting more than a century ago, whose original publication appeared in an old and outdated German script—why should the *Memoirs* and now also the *Letters* be of any interest, much less inspiration, today? Why, indeed, has there even been an uptick of interest in the last decades? I will not provide the catalogue of reasons here, but just offer a smattering of thoughts, like a trail of crumbs to entice further travel, as we journey with Sayyida Salme's writings toward greater awareness and understanding.

It is often said that Sayyida Salme was ahead of her time, and being the first Arab woman to ever publish a book already puts her in that category. People remark on her proclivity to do the unthinkable, and also her ability to question social constructs and challenge common tropes. She had her own notions and tested limits, not necessarily because she wanted to, but often because of what she had become: an infidel, a single mother, a pawn, a caricature. But what made her so prescient, I would say, is her uncanny and uniquely situated ability—through the life she led and the piquant observations she made—to tap into currents and questions that still dog us today.

Having been deep in these translations over the past several years while preparing my two books, I am particularly prone to finding her relevance wherever I look. But really, I can hardly scan the headlines without finding some news story or commentary that echoes her life and concerns. My pile of "relevance" topics runneth over—from the writings of 2021 Nobel Prize-winner Abdulrazak Gurnah (whose modern fiction is an amazing overlay to Sayyida Salme's time and place); to the Taliban's push to train female doctors (something Sayyida Salme advocated in her time) as a small exception to (and necessitated by) their appalling subjugation of women; to the proliferating examples of backlash against minorities and the politically-motivated "cancel culture" responses (including Hamburg's rejection of its previously-designated Emily-Ruete-Platz); to royals that choose to give up their royal stations (Princess Martha Louise of Norway, Prince Harry of England); to reports of PEN America's Manifesto on Literary Translation (espousing principles that were sorely lacking in Sayyida Salme's time); and much more. The range of her experiences and the precious detail of her accounts refract one theme after another that still pertains.

On Inspiration

As a writer myself, I cannot consider the story of Sayyida Salme without being struck by the power of the pen. It began with some combination of intelligence and audacity, guts and gumption, perhaps even a drive to compete with the boys, when she secretly taught herself to write in Arabic using homemade ink on a camel shoulder blade. If she was testing limits, making trouble, or subverting authority, at least she was writing holy verses from the Koran. How subversive can that be? Or perhaps she was just indulging in creative exploration, since she could already read and recite much of the Koran, and how do you undo the learning once it is learned? Even though she stunned those around her and got into passing trouble when it came out, the act of making literacy part of her identity enabled a degree of self-expression and empowerment that shaped the rest of her life.

I try to picture a teenager, having first been scolded for writing, but then validated and encouraged, even expected, to write one letter after another to serve the cause. In supporting Barghash with his coup attempt, Sayyida Salme weaponized her pen at age 15 before she learned to write for herself and reveal her own sense of the world. As she tells us in her Preface and Afterword, writing the *Memoirs* for her children was an act of love, and publishing the *Memoirs* for an international audience was an act of truth-telling. But her *Letters*, did she write them to remember, for the record, or perhaps even to soothe her soul? We do not know, but as we read her words now, her voice is clear, her tone is pronounced, and her self is amply expressed. Coming fresh off the success of her *Memoirs*, she must have known she had more to write. And in so doing, this literary legacy has not only let her "contribute my share,"[111] but also illuminates the importance, across the ages, of words and writing as a way both to be oneself and to reveal oneself.

Such tools of liberation have heightened importance in societies where voices are tamped down and expression is caged in. Women, in particular, keep bumping up against the bars of the cage, of which Sayyida Salme gives us so many examples in her time, both in Zanzibar and Germany. We can dwell, for example, on that awful moment when she was first turned away from the hospital where her husband lay dying, or less obviously when no one moved to help her get to his burial—as the cultural tropes go, better keep the

---

111 *Memoirs*, Afterword, p. 229. Given the author's explicit mission, including her goal of "above all, … removing many misconceptions and distortions current about the East," it is more than ironic that the author's original German has been so mistranslated. My new translations, written to be as accurate and consistent with her originals as possible, seek to rectify the distortions from historical translations. For comparisons to make the point, see www.sayyidasalme.com.

women away, they are too emotional, too hysterical, too embarrassing, too uncontrollable, whatever the thinking.

We also see who built the cage. Whether imposed as the virtual mummification women had to endure to protect men in Zanzibar or disclosed in low décolletés that flaunted bodies to entertain men in Hamburg, social mores were typically designed from a male point of view.[112] Indeed, if we look closely enough, this difference in attire readily maps onto the difference between the Western monogamy and Eastern polygamy that Sayyida Salme so bitingly describes: "I am tempted to say that the only difference between an Oriental wife and a European wife appears to be that the first has knowledge of the number, as well as the nature and character, of her rivals, while the other is kept in loving ignorance."[113] Whether the women were massively or scantily dressed, both the Zanzibari Sultanate and the Hamburg elite were patriarchal societies that had their private codes, their conservative principles, their closed circles, and their need to keep up appearances—where a dangerously errant or exotically vagrant princess had little room.

A society that likes its order, this is how we do it, and a patriarchy that likes male hierarchy, this is how *we* do it, are apt to respect—and fear and other—women to the point of abnegation. In her day, Sayyida Salme had to advocate, persuade, and persist, but as an act of resistance, she could also write—and thus let us feel her pain, contemplate the cost, and consider our own experiences. How striking that this early transgression became a lifelong lifeline: "Oh, how grateful I have been over the years for a decision that enabled me, however imperfectly, to correspond directly with my loyal friends in my distant homeland!"[114] Thank goodness she could and did reach for her pen.

This commentary is perhaps a bit unfair in that we have only her writings, not those of her husband, Heinrich. He surely had views, but did not share the literary craft, and his life was cut so short. The mind wanders, and we can wonder, what on earth was he thinking? Sayyida Salme's unwavering respect, appreciation, and love for him stand as a pillar across all her pages, and that I would take at face value, as genuine as the rest of what she writes. But there are clues that he, too, did not quite fit in. He was his father's first child, born to a mother who died when he had just turned four. When his father remarried

---

112 My thanks to Anita Keizers at the NINO (Netherlands Institute for the Near East) in Leiden for our stimulating conversation, in which she also shared this thought.
113 *Memoirs*, p. 110.
114 *Memoirs*, p. 36.

two years later, and started a second family with five more children,[115] Heinrich may have been the odd one out.

Having grown up in a great port city, Heinrich was still a teenager when he apprenticed with Hansing & Co. and all of 18 when he became one of their agents in Zanzibar.[116] There he lived a trader's life for almost a decade before he met his wife. Who was there to teach him "proper" behavior, if he had in fact wanted to learn? From a Hamburg perspective, being part of elite society, but not so high up that he could easily break the rules, he was surely expected to marry a respectable local. From a Zanzibari perspective, laying a hand on a royal daughter was the height of insolence, not to mention endangering her life more than his. Even after Heinrich's perceived transgressions toward the Sultan's sister, and clear indications from the Sultan that this German was no longer welcome, Heinrich still insisted that he had violated no rules and demanded, all the way up to Chancellor Bismarck, his right to engage in Zanzibari trade. The stand-off was resolved when both Heinrich and Sultan Madjid died tragically young in the same year.[117] Would that we had more details of Heinrich's life, seemingly another fish out of water.

Yet, this is what happens when people move. This is the confusion and collision of cultures when people leave their homelands. The lines were starker and the contrasts greater in the mid-nineteenth century, before the homogenizing forces of our flattening world. Still today, though, the immigrant experience challenges both the people on the move and the people they are moving to. It is not hard to foresee a future where climate change, social upheaval, and forces beyond our imagining will propel more movement, and mixing and matching, that put a premium on our ability to be open, tolerant, and humane. It is not hard to see history rhyme.

All of which reminds me why I do the professional work I do, my many years as a lawyer helping build international partnerships at the World Bank and beyond. It lets me be part of the international community's effort to find a better balance between developed and developing countries.[118] The tendency throughout history has been so vertical—as with colonialism, autocracy, royalty, slavery,

---

115 We are fortunate to be friends with Ursula Luther, a kindred spirit and namesake of my mother Ursula, and a direct descendant of one of Sayyida Salme's in-laws, Heinrich's half-sister Sarah Maria (Ruete) Rothenbücher. She provided some of these details, along with a detailed Ruete family tree.
116 Heinz Schneppen, "Jena: Emily Ruete, eine Prinzessin aus Sansibar," in *Kolonialismus hierzulande. Eine Spurensuche in Deutschland*, p. 222 (U. van der Heyden, J. Zeller 2008). But see E. van Donzel, p. 12, which states that Heinrich was in Zanzibar already at age 16.
117 H. Schneppen, *Briefe*, p. 151–52.
118 This distinction between "developed" and "developing" countries still largely tracks the old Oriental-Occidental/East-West/South-North divide of Sayyida Salme's time.

war,[119] and plunder—and the world is still young in trying to organize itself horizontally. Whether, for example, through more democracy within countries or more consensus-based platforms across countries, the ability to engage peer-to-peer as citizens and as sovereign nations remains a work in progress.[120]

In her Omani father and Circassian mother, Sayyida Salme herself embodied a remarkable alignment between the heft of Omani colonialism and the effect of Russian genocidal incursion. Although she ended up at the top of the vertical, she could just as easily have ended up at the bottom (witness slavery in the American South). But vertical it was, and vertical it stayed, albeit with a twist. Even though she came from a great Omani dynasty, arguably as prosperous as any European nation of the time, the trip from South to North flipped her status from princess and privilege to exotic and primitive.[121] We may ponder some of Sayyida Salme's descriptions, and rightfully criticize some of her statements, but ideally not before we appreciate her views as an exposition and defense of her own highly-developed society and culture with legitimate local interests.

Her title, *Letters to the Homeland*, reminds us that she came from both a home and a land: a place, a people, a culture, a society.[122] What a different life she would have had with less hierarchy in the harem and less verticality in the international arena. It is not a question of being equals—Sayyida Salme was unlikely ever to fully conform, nor should anyone have to—but it is a question of more equivalent footing, of being horizontal more than vertical in relation to each other, whether as individuals or countries. And that is one more way in which we might be inspired.

> Let history surprise you, let her story inspire you—
> let her authentic voice speak to you.

---

119 Having come from a warring culture, including a father who killed to succeed his father and was venerated for his military accomplishments, Sayyida Salme was remarkably anti-war: "For . . . people who have no association with Christianity and know of the peaceful, love-thy-neighbor teachings of Jesus only through books and stories, it must appear totally incongruous to watch how its adherents seek to outdo each other in who can invent the deadliest and most *en gros* annihilating weapon. . . . [Y]ou, however, in your simplicity, if you were to consider all these arts that they call progress here, were you to see all of it and everything that goes with it, I am entirely sure you would call them—simply satanic." (above at pages 42–43)

120 A favorite example of such a horizontal effort is the 2005 Paris Declaration on Aid Effectiveness, which espouses principles like developing country ownership based on country priorities, corresponding alignment by donor countries of their support, and mutual accountability for results.

121 Anyone who studies Sayyida Salme's life immediately recognizes the contradiction of someone who was both a subject and object of the racism that was so widespread at the time.

122 The inscription on Sayyida Salme's gravestone is a fitting verse from Theodor Fontane's 1854 "Archibald Douglas," about an exiled soul who found his way back home: *Der ist in tiefster Seele treu, wer die Heimat liebt wie Du.* (Whosoever loves his homeland as you do, is loyal to the core.) Although Sayyida Salme never returned for good, she was laid to rest with a small sack of sand from Zanzibar that was found among her belongings.

From her pen to mine,

her voice to mine,

this quest to self-express:

·•·

words that echo over time,

pain to prose in lines that rhyme,

from her to me to you to us.

Andrea Emily Stumpf
September 14, 2023

The children, Rosa, Said, and Antonie, in Dresden probably around 1873.

The children, Said, Antonie, and Rosa, in Dresden in 1875.

The children, Antonie, Said, and Rosa, in Berlin in 1879.

The author's son Said, who usually also got special solo poses.

The son Said in traditional attire in 1875.

The daughter Antonie in traditional attire in the mid-1880s.

LIST OF ABBREVIATIONS

Abbreviations		Pages
B.	half-brother Sultan Barghash	60, 71
Doctor C.	unknown identity	48
Madame C.	unknown identity	5
Ch.	half-sister Chole	27, 58
Doctor G.	unknown identity	52
H.	likely brother-in-law Hermann Ruete	105
Cousin H.	unknown identity	21
Dr. K.	unknown identity	89
L.	unknown location	103
M.	half-brother Sultan Madjid	25, 60, 66,
M.	possibly half-sister Mettle or Meje	71
M.	couple Mr. and Mrs. Bonaventura Mass	6
Madame M.	Mrs. Bonaventura Mass	5, 6, 31
Doctor R.	unknown identity	46, 47
S.	son Said (later Rudolph Said-Ruete)	98–102, 111–119
T.	daughter Tony (Antonie)	14
Baroness T.	Baroness von Tettau	94
Pastor T.	unknown identity	54

TIMELINE

These dates have been collected from various sources, some more substantiated than others. This list is meant to provide an approximate overview and should not be considered a fully verified historical record.

1698	The Omanis defeat the Portuguese on the island of Zanzibar
1806	Sayyid Said becomes Sultan of Oman
1822	Sayyid Said signs the Moresby Treaty with Britain to end the export of East African slaves to Christian colonies
1834	British Slavery Abolition Act frees all slaves held by British subjects (including from India) on Zanzibar and elsewhere
1837	Sayyid Said defeats the Portuguese in Mombasa
March 10, 1839	Rudolph Heinrich Ruete (called Heinrich) is born in Hamburg
1840	Sayyid Said moves his primary residence from Muscat to Zanzibar
August 30, 1844	Sayyida Salme is born in Bet il Mtoni in Zanzibar
1845	Sayyid Said signs the Hamerton Treaty with the British limiting slave trading to routes between Zanzibar and East Africa
1851	Sayyida Salme and her mother move to Bet il Wataro
1853	Sayyida Salme and her mother move to Bet il Tani
1853	Hansing & Co. of Hamburg opens shop in Zanzibar
1856	Sayyid Said dies; Madjid steps in as Sultan of Zanzibar

1856	Sayyida Salme is declared of age and inherits her portion of the estate
1857	Heinrich Ruete moves to Zanzibar as an agent of Hansing & Co., later becoming a partner in Koll & Ruete and then his own Ruete & Co.
1859	Sayyida Salme's mother dies in a cholera outbreak
1859	Barghash attempts his coup to replace Sultan Madjid
1860 ~	Sayyida Salme moves to her plantation Kisimbani
April 1861	Under arbitration by British Lord Canning, Zanzibar and Oman formally settle claims and divide rule
1862/3 ~	Sayyida Salme rents Bububu and moves to the seashore
1864/5 ~	Sayyida Salme moves to Stone Town because Madjid asks to give Bububu to the new British Consul
1865	Sayyida Salme meets Heinrich Ruete as a neighbor in Stone Town
August 9, 1866	Sayyida Salme makes an unsuccessful attempt to leave Zanzibar
August 24/25, 1866	Sayyida Salme escapes Zanzibar on the HMS *Highflyer* to Aden, the night before *Siku ya Mwaka*, the Swahili New Year
December 7, 1866	Sayyida Salme's firstborn Heinrich is born in Aden
April 1, 1867	The infant Heinrich is baptized in the Anglican Church in Aden
May 30, 1867	Heinrich Ruete arrives in Aden from the Seychelles; Sayyida Salme becomes Christian and is baptized Emily; Sayyida Salme marries Heinrich Ruete; the new couple and their son leave Aden for Hamburg via the Red Sea and Marseille-Lyon-Paris
June 24, 1867	The infant Heinrich dies on the train between Lyon and Paris, as certified in Paris by the child's father on June 25 and again by the child's grandfather in Hamburg on June 30 (thank you to Fridjof Gutendorf)

Timeline

June 24, 1867	The young couple arrives in Hamburg and takes up residence at Schöne Aussicht 29, Uhlenhorst
March 24, 1868	Antonie (Tony) Ghawka Ruete is born (who later became Antonie Brandeis)
April 13, 1869	Said Ruete is born (who later changed his name to Rudolph Said-Ruete)
Summer 1869	Sayyida Salme and her husband travel briefly to Copenhagen
April 16, 1870	Rosalie (Rosa) Ghuza Ruete is born (who later became Rosalie Troemer)
1870	Sultan Madjid sends gifts by steamer to Sayyida Salme, which are never received
July 1870	The Franco-Prussian War begins and lasts into 1871
August 6, 1870	Heinrich Ruete dies a few days after a tragic tram accident
October 7, 1870	Sultan Madjid dies in Zanzibar; Barghash becomes Sultan
Winter 1870/71	The Zanzibari warship *Ilmedjidi* docks in Hamburg
Spring 1871	Sayyida Salme moves to a cheaper Hamburg residence, Blücherstrasse 11 (now Heinrich-Hertz-Strasse 112) (per Fridjof Gutendorf)
1871	The German Reich under Bismarck is established
May 1, 1872	Sayyida Salme becomes a citizen of Hamburg and thus Germany
1872/3	Sayyida Salme moves with the children from Hamburg to Dresden
June 5, 1873	Sultan Barghash signs a treaty with the British to end all slave trading
1873	Sayyida Salme finally gets full visibility of her deteriorated finances

1874	Sayyida Salme moves to a cheaper residence in Dresden
Summer 1875	Sayyida Salme travels to London to meet with Sultan Barghash, without success
1875/77 ~	Sayyida Salme begins writing her *Memoirs*
1877	Sayyida Salme moves again, this time from Dresden to Rudolstadt
1877	The children find out at school that their mother is a princess
1879	Sayyida Salme moves from Rudolstadt to Berlin, Genthiner Strasse
October 1881	Sayyida Salme's son Said joins the Bensberg Cadet Academy; Sayyida Salme and her children move temporarily to nearby Cologne
1882	Sayyida Salme returns with her daughters to Berlin and takes up residence at Potsdamer Strasse 70a
1883	Sayyida Salme writes Sultan Barghash directly to reconcile
Summer/fall 1885	Sayyida Salme returns to Zanzibar with her three children under German military escort
October 1885	Sultan Barghash provides a small sum to settle claims that Sayyida Salme declines to accept
Spring 1888	Sayyida Salme returns to Zanzibar, this time with Rosa only
1888	The authorized English translation of the *Memoiren* appears in London
1888	A bootleg copy of the English translation appears in New York City
November 1888	Sayyida Salme leaves Zanzibar on a down note
December 1888	Sayyida Salme settles in Jaffa (now southern Tel Aviv)

1890	Sayyida Salme visits Berlin
1892	Sayyida Salme moves to Beirut
1897	Sayyida Salme visits Berlin
1898	Antonie marries Eugen Brandeis and moves to the Marshall Islands, where he was appointed governor of the German protectorate
1900	Sayyida Salme visits Said in Cairo
September 16, 1901	Said's wedding to Maria Theresa Mathias of the Mond family in Berlin; Sayyida Salme attends
September 17, 1902	Rosa marries Captain Martin Gottlob Reinhold Troemer (later Major, then Major General)
1905	A French translation of the *Memoiren* appears in Paris
1907	An unauthorized English translation of the *Memoiren* by Lionel Strachey appears in New York City
1914	Sayyida Salme leaves Beirut to move in with Rosa and her husband at Bülowstrasse 17, Bromberg (now Bydgoszcz in Poland)
1920	Sayyida Salme moves with Rosa and now retired Major General Troemer to Gartenstrasse 4, Jena
February 29, 1924	Sayyida Salme dies in Jena, in Rosa's home, of double pneumonia
1924	Sayyida Salme is buried on the Ruete family plot, next to her husband, in the Ohlsdorf Cemetery in Hamburg

1866. Abreise von Zanzibar nach Aden

1867. Abreise von Aden nach Suez, Cairo, Alexandrien, Marseille & Hamburg 24 Juni.

1872. Reise von Hamburg nach Berlin zu Staatssekr. von Bülow.

1873. Umzug von Hamburg nach Dresden.

1875. Reise nach London

1877. Umzug nach Rudolstadt.

1879. Umzug von Rudolstadt nach Berlin (Genthiner Str.)

1882. Nach Cöln (wegen Said)

1885. Reise mit dem Deutschen Kaiser nach Zanzibar.

1888. Zweite Reise nach Zanzibar, Cypern, Jaffa ... [illegible] nach Hornstr. 8.

Handwritten timeline from the author.

1890. Reise nach Berlin, Calainths.
1892. Reise nach Mailand, Genua, Port Said, Cairo & Beirut.
1897. Reise nach Berlin (b. Schreier) & zurück nach Beirut mit Jarry.
1898. Im April Rosa & E. nach Beirut.
1898. Im Herbst Port Said nach Beirut.
1900. Reise ich allein p. Said nach Cairo.
1901. Reise ich mit Rosa p. Said Suez nach Berlin
1901. Juli, August, kam Jarry mit Gretchen nach Deutschland.
1902. Reise ich im Januar von Berlin nach Beirut zurück.

Tucked away by her son in one of his collected books.

LIST OF IMAGES

Special thanks are due to Alexander von Brand and his family for the extraordinary gift of preserving and sharing many of the family photographs appearing for the first time in public in these pages. They tell a story in and of themselves, and it has been a joy to lay them out in their full succession here.

[Front cover] Same photograph as [xiv] below.

[iv] Front cover of *Memoirs of an Arabian Princess: An Accurate Translation of Her Authentic Voice* (2022), by Andrea Emily Stumpf, ISBN 978-1-732397-3-8.

[viii–xi] Four studio photographs of the author in traditional Omani/Zanzibari attire by photographer H.F. Plate, taken in Hamburg in 1868, not long after her arrival in Germany; from the Leiden University Libraries at Or. 27.135 D1.

[xii–xiii] Two studio photographs of the author in German attire by photographer W. Breuning, taken in Hamburg around 1868; from the Leiden University Libraries at Or. 27.135 D2(3) and D2(2).

[xiv] Studio photograph of the author by photographer J.C. Schaarwächter, taken in Berlin in March 1888, according to the handwritten notation; from the Leiden University Libraries at Or. 27.135 D5.

[xv] Studio photograph of the author by photographer J.C. Schaarwächter, undated but presumably from the same 1888 studio session as the prior photograph; provided by Alexander von Brand from his family collection.

[xvi] Studio photograph of the author dated December 1908, according to a handwritten notation ("XII/1908"); the same photograph in duplicate is accompanied by a photograph of the author's son Rudolph Said-Ruete and a handwritten dedication dated October 1924 from Rudolph to Professor Christiaan Snouck Hurgronje ("Herrn Professor Dr. C. Snouck Hurgronje das Bild meiner ihm in aufrichtiger Wertschätzung verbunden gewesenen Mutter, Frau Emily Ruete/Prinzessin von Oman und Zanzibar, freundschaftlich zugeeignet – RSaidRuete"), apparently presented as a gift following her death; from the Leiden University Libraries at Or. 27.135 D7.

List of Images

[xvii] Studio photograph of the author, undated and unattributed, but presumably from the same 1908 studio session as the prior photograph; provided by Alexander von Brand from his family collection.

[xviii] Photograph of the author, undated but presumably taken during the period from 1892 to 1914 when the author lived in Lebanon; the handwritten name on the photograph is misspelled (it should be Ruete, not Reute), while "Libanon" is the German spelling of Lebanon; provided by Alexander von Brand from his family collection.

[xix] Photograph of the author, dated July 1914, the year she left Beirut to return to Germany, and taken in Bromberg (now Bydgoszcz, since 1920 under the Treaty of Versailles), where she moved in with her daughter Rosa and husband Major General Martin Troemer; from an album compiled by the author's son Rudolph Said-Ruete in the Leiden University Libraries at Or. 27.135 H5.

[xxvi–xxvii] Excerpts from the author's three handwritten notebooks (I, II, and III) containing her original "Briefe nach der Heimat" totaling over six hundred pages, in each case showing the cover page plus the first three pages; from the Leiden University Libraries at Or. 27.135 A3–5. These notebooks will soon become available for public access as digital copies, in part to safeguard the very fragile originals. A useful additional reference point is the collection guide and inventory located at ubl649, which provides historical background and itemizes the materials in the "Sayyida Salma [sic] (Emily Ruete) and Rudolph Said Ruete" archive.

[xxviii] First page of an early typewritten copy of the author's "Briefe nach der Heimat;" provided by Alexander von Brand from his family collection.

[xxix] First page of an upgraded typewritten copy of the author's "Briefe nach der Heimat" that is part of the compilation described under page [1] below; from the Leiden University Libraries at Or. 6281.

[xxx] Studio photograph of the author taken by photographer H.F. Plate in Hamburg around 1868, not long after her arrival in Germany, and used as the frontispiece for her 1886 publication of the *Memoiren einer arabischen Prinzessin*; from the translator's family collection.

[1] Cover page of a compilation of the author's legacy writings prepared as typed manuscripts by the family after the author's death in 1924 and formally presented as her "Literarischer Nachlass" (Literary Estate) to various institutions by the author's son Rudolph, including to Professor Christiaan Snouck Hurgronje and his Leiden-based Oriental Institute in 1928–29; the

compilation consists of the "Nachtrag zu den Memoiren" (Addendum to the Memoirs) and "Syrische Sitten und Gebräuche" (Syrian Customs and Practices), in addition to the "Briefe nach der Heimat"; located in the Leiden University Libraries at Or. 6281.

[3] Illustration by Max S. Stumpf, © 2023.

[7] Steel engraving of Hamburg from the mid-1880s, including in the center the Jungfernstieg; published by A.H. Payne Dresden & Leipzig.

[15] Illustration by Max S. Stumpf, © 2023.

[18] Studio photograph of the author's husband Heinrich Ruete, with an imprint of "E. Bieber, Hamburg" and handwritten "1863" on the back; this date is somewhat in doubt, since Heinrich was in Zanzibar during most of this time; see also regarding the photograph described under page [56] below; provided by Alexander von Brand from his family collection.

[19] Studio photograph of the author in Germany that was paired with the prior photograph; undated and unlabeled, but likely taken around 1868; provided by Alexander von Brand from his family collection; a second copy of this same photograph taken by photographer H.F. Plate, likely the original photographer, is located in the Leiden University Libraries at Or. 27.135 D2(1).

[28] Illustration by Max S. Stumpf, © 2023.

[43] Stereograph of a French battlefield entitled "Red fields of slaughter sloping down to ruin's black abyss," taken during World War I between 1914 and 1918 and published in 1923 by the Keystone View Company; from the Library of Congress Prints and Photograph Division, call number Lot 14008, no. 175 [P&P].

[46] Horse-drawn tram in Hamburg from the late 1860s; photograph featured in an article by Matthias Schmoock, "So fuhr die erste Strassenbahn in Hamburg" (This is How the First Streetcar in Hamburg Ran), August 13, 2016, in the *Hamburger Abendblatt* (photograph credit Hochbahn).

[50] "Ansicht von Sansibar" (View of Zanzibar) on page 3 of the article "Sansibar und Bagamoyo" in the January 1874 edition of the *Illustrierte Monatschrift* (Illustrated Monthly) of the Catholic Mission; with thanks to Hans van de Velde for generously sharing.

List of Images

[53] Illustration by Max S. Stumpf, © 2023.

[56] Undated studio photograph of Heinrich Ruete from photographer W. Breuning in Hamburg; this may be a set with the W. Breuning photographs of the author on pages xii and xiii above, but also appears to be from the same studio session as the photograph on page 18 above taken by E. Bieber; because a handwritten "Copie" appears on the back of this photograph, it may be that E. Bieber was the original photographer and W. Breuning reissued the photograph in connection with the author's subsequent studio session; from Leiden University Libraries at Or. 27.135 D3.

[57] Studio photograph of the author's husband Heinrich Ruete, taken by photographer E. Bieber in Hamburg sometime in 1869–70 (undated, but noting exhibits attended in 1865, 1868, and 1869); with the notation "Für Tony" (For Tony) on the back; provided by Alexander von Brand from his family collection.

[62] Undated colored lithograph of Sayyid Madjid bin Said, Sultan of Zanzibar from 1856–1870; from Leiden University Libraries at Or. 27.135 D18.

[63] Undated colored lithograph of Sayyid Barghash bin Said, Sultan of Zanzibar from 1870–1888; from Leiden University Libraries at Or. 27.135 D21.

[67] Painting of the ship that became the *Ilmedjidi* or "El Majidi," taken from J.L. Carvel, *Stephen of Linthouse: A Record of Two Hundred Years of Shipbuilding 1750–1950*, pp. 40–41 (1950), and fortuitously provided by Thomas Theye, Bremen, who contacted me during his research and alerted me to this ship's fascinating twists and turns. The formidable vessel with its characteristic smokestack was built in Glasgow and began life in 1863 as the tea clipper *Sea King* before taking on a second life in the American Civil War as the feared Confederate raider CSS *Shenandoah* that demolished Yankee whaling fleets wherever it could find them. After the war ended, the ship was surrendered in Liverpool and later sold to Sultan Madjid, who turned it into a Zanzibari warship. Wrecked in the April 1872 cyclone that devastated Zanzibar, the ship was soon headed to Bombay for repairs when it started to leak and then sank. Officers and crew dispersed in several boats, but many perished, according to a letter from Lieutenant Arthur Philpotts, HM Ship Briton at Zanzibar on December 18, 1872, a copy of which resides in the Hamburg City Archives at 111–1_46996, Annex 2, again helpfully provided by Theye. Theye also reveals the even more astonishing story of how photographs taken by Carl Dammann in 1870 of the *Ilmedjidi*'s crew were heralded, sold, and scrutinized as racial specimens. See Thomas Theye, "Im Spinnennetz: Karl Ernst von Baer und Otto Buchner, Adolf

Bastian und Rudolf Virchow, Carl Dammann und die 'Photographiesammlung' der Berliner Gesellschaft für Anthropologie, Ethnologie und Urgeschichte," in *Mitteilungen der Berliner Gesellschaft für Anthropologie, Ethnologie und Urgeschichte*, Vol. 43, pp. 102–08 (2022).

[70] Sketched portrait of the author's father, Sayyid Said, Sultan of Oman and ruler of Zanzibar from 1806–1856, with a handwritten notation from the author's son Rudolph; the image was glued by Rudolph into W.H. Ingram's "Said bin Sultan: An Appreciation" from 1926, which Rudolph had inserted into his copy of Shaik Mansur's *History of Seyd Said, Sultan of Muscat* (1819); this type of careful compilation of annotated materials is typical of Rudolph's 600+ book collection that he gave to the Oriental Institute in Leiden; located in Leiden University Libraries at SR 432.

[79] Steel engraving from the mid-1800s of Dresden scenes; published by A.H. Payne Dresden & Leipzig.

[87] Illustration by Max S. Stumpf, © 2023.

[93] Steel engraving from the mid-1800s of Rudolstadt; as printed on the bottom, "Aus der Kunstanst. d. Bibliogr. Inst. in Hildbh." (Hildburghausen).

[97] Illustration by Max S. Stumpf, © 2023.

[107] Steel engraving from the mid-1800s of Berlin scenes; published by A.H. Payne Dresden & Leipzig.

[115] Colored lithograph of Bensberg, including the cadet academy to which the author's son was assigned; used as a postcard for correspondence within Germany in 1899.

[121] Locations where Sayyida Salme lived in Germany (including one in what is now Poland); by Max S. Stumpf, © 2023.

[122] The only photograph of the author and her husband together with their children, in this case Antonie and Said, by photographer W. Breuning in Hamburg; with 1870 on the background cardstock handwritten by the author's son (this was likely taken before April 1870, when the author was pregnant with Rosa); from Leiden University Libraries at Or. 27.135 D4.

[123] Unlabeled studio photograph of the author and her three children, Said (in the chair), Rosa (on the lap), and Antonie; taken after the author's husband died, probably in the first half of 1871; provided by Alexander von Brand from his family collection.

List of Images

[124] Studio photograph of the author and her children, Rosa (14), Said (15), and Antonie (16), by photographer J.C. Schaarwächter; with "Herbst 1884" (fall 1884) written on the background cardstock; provided by Alexander von Brand from his family collection.

[125] Studio photograph of the author and her children, Antonie, Said, and Rosa, taken by photographer W. Höffert; although undated, it appears that Ernst Friedrich Wilhelm Hugo Höffert had studios in Berlin from 1885 to 1900; the four coats of arms reflect his various appointments as court photographer; from the translator's family collection.

[128] The author's signed dedication to her son in a copy of her 1886 *Memoiren einer arabischen Prinzessin*; from www.omanisilver.com by permission of Hielke van der Wijk, whose significant collection of artifacts from and related to Oman is accompanied by thoughtfully researched descriptions.

[130] Excerpt from a carbon copy of a letter dated October 14, 1928, from the author's son Rudolph Said-Ruete, in which he protests Sir Arthur H. Hardinge's characterization of the author in his book *A Diplomatist in the East* (1928), this example being just one of many errors about the author that appeared in the book; Hardinge died before the publisher took responsibility, and no corrections were made as no further editions were published; this is one of several letters placed by Rudolph in the referenced book that is part of his bestowed collection, located at Leiden University Libraries at SR 289.

[146] Studio photograph of the author's children Rosa, Said, and Antonie, undated but probably around 1873 after the family moved to Dresden; taken by photographer Wilhelm Hoffmann in Dresden; provided by Alexander von Brand from his family collection.

[147] Studio photograph of the author's children Said, Antonie, and Rosa taken by photographer Carl Arazim from Dresden in 1875; provided by Alexander von Brand from his family collection.

[148] Studio photograph of the author's children Antonie (11), Said (10), and Rosa (9) taken by photographer J. van Ronzelen from Berlin with a handwritten date of October 1879 on the background cardstock; provided by Alexander von Brand from his family collection.

[149] Four studio photographs of the author's son Said, posing alone: (i) taken during the same studio session as page 146 above (top left), (ii) studio photograph with a handwritten date of November 1875 on the background cardstock (bottom left), (iii) taken during the same studio session as page 124

above (top right), and (iv) taken by photographer L. Haase & Co. from Berlin, undated; most family studio sessions appear to have included solo poses by the son, but not the daughters; provided by Alexander von Brand from his family collection.

[150] Studio photograph of the author's son Said in traditional Omani/Zanzibari attire, including an Omani kummah cap typically worn by men, taken during the same studio session as page 147 above; provided by Alexander von Brand from his family collection.

[151] Studio photograph of the author's eldest daughter in traditional attire, including the same Omani kummah cap that Said wore in the prior photograph about ten years earlier; taken by photographer L.A. Vassel (Gustav Leon Alfred Vassel) from Berlin and undated, but probably in the mid-1880s, around the time of the family's 1885 trip to Zanzibar; provided by Alexander von Brand from his family collection.

[158–59] Timeline handwritten by the author and enclosed by her son Rudolph inside E. Sachau, *Über eine arabische Chronik aus Zanzibar* (1898), one of the books that is part of Rudolph's bestowed collection, located at Leiden University Libraries at SR 631.

[166] Image imprinted on the cover of an album of family photographs compiled by Rudolph and preserved as part of his special collection; located at Leiden University Libraries Or. 27.135 H5.

[Back cover] Left: Same photograph as [xi] above. Right: Studio photograph of the author by photographer Progress-Photographie, with a handwritten February 1, 1915 date on the framing cardstock; provided by Alexander von Brand from his family collection.

www.ingramcontent.com/pod-product-compliance
Lightning Source LLC
Chambersburg PA
CBHW052140070526
44585CB00017B/1904